Drug Use and Abuse

Editor: Tracy Biram

Volume 373

First published by Independence Educational Publishers
The Studio, High Green
Great Shelford
Cambridge CB22 5EG
England

ISBN-13: 978 1 86168 830 9

Printed in Great Britain

Zenith Print Group

Contents

Chapter 1: Drugs Overview

Chapter 2: Drugs and the Law

Chapter 3: Addiction and Rehab

Introduction

Drug Use and Abuse is Volume 373 in the ISSUES series. The aim of the series is to offer current, diverse information about important issues in our world, from a UK perspective.

ABOUT DRUG USE AND ABUSE

According to recent statistics 9.4% of UK adults aged 16 to 59 have taken illicit drugs in the last year. In 2019 the UK saw its highest ever levels of drug related deaths – making the UK the country with the highest number in Europe, three times higher than the average. This book explores legal and illegal drugs and the dangerous effects they can have on individuals and society as a whole. We also look at UK drug laws and the resources available to help those suffering with an addiction.

OUR SOURCES

Titles in the **ISSUES** series are designed to function as educational resource books, providing a balanced overview of a specific subject.

The information in our books is comprised of facts, articles and opinions from many different sources, including:

- Newspaper reports and opinion pieces
- Website factsheets
- Magazine and journal articles
- Statistics and surveys
- Government reports
- Literature from special interest groups.

A NOTE ON CRITICAL EVALUATION

Because the information reprinted here is from a number of different sources, readers should bear in mind the origin of the text and whether the source is likely to have a particular bias when presenting information (or when conducting their research). It is hoped that, as you read about the many aspects of the issues explored in this book, you will critically evaluate the information presented.

It is important that you decide whether you are being presented with facts or opinions. Does the writer give a biased or unbiased report? If an opinion is being expressed, do you agree with the writer? Is there potential bias to the 'facts' or statistics behind an article?

ASSIGNMENTS

In the back of this book, you will find a selection of assignments designed to help you engage with the articles you have been reading and to explore your own opinions. Some tasks will take longer than others and there is a mixture of design, writing and research-based activities that you can complete alone or in a group.

FURTHER RESEARCH

At the end of each article we have listed its source and a website that you can visit if you would like to conduct your own research. Please remember to critically evaluate any sources that you consult and consider whether the information you are viewing is accurate and unbiased.

Useful Websites

www.digital.nhs.uk
www.getsurrey.co.uk
www.gov.scot
www.gov.uk
www.healtheuropa.eu
www.independent.co.uk
www.inews.co.uk
www.libertyhouseclinic.co.uk
www.news-decoder.com
www.nhs.uk
www.nrscotland.gov.uk
www.shoutoutuk.org
www.telegraph.co.uk
www.theconversation.com
www.theguardian.com
www.ukat.co.uk

Chapter 1

Drugs Overview

Drug addiction and abuse

Drug addiction is an illness; it is a complex brain disorder characterised by the compulsive consumption of a substance of abuse, most often illicit drugs, despite the awareness that doing so has detrimental consequences.

The consumption of addictive substances of abuse is both intrinsically rewarding (that is, the effects of that consumption are seen by the addict as being enjoyable and desirable – even if simultaneously the addict may dearly wish to stop consuming their substance of choice) and reinforcing (i.e. it makes the person consuming the drug wish to keep consuming it over and over again).

A person may be either physically addicted, psychologically addicted, or both, depending on which specific substance they consume (only some drugs are physically addictive), and the response of the addict's body and mind to the presence of the drug (and its absence from the system upon cessation of use) will vary accordingly.

However, in the cases of both psychological and physical addiction, the addict will crave their substance of abuse, and procuring and consuming it will come to dominate their daily routine, their thought processes, and eventually their entire lives – often at terrible cost to their life prospects and circumstances, their relationships, their self-esteem, and their physical and mental health.

What is drug addiction?

Addiction is defined by the US National Institutes for Health (NIH) as 'a chronic, relapsing brain disease that is characterized by compulsive drug seeking and use, despite harmful consequences'.

The flipside of the coin is that not consuming the drug has negative consequences – in the short term – in terms of the way in which the brain's reward system responds, and – in the case of physical addiction (or drug dependency) – in terms of how the addict's body responds to the absence of the substance on which it has become dependent.

Both physical and psychological addiction can lead to withdrawal – the manifestation of often extremely unpleasant (and in some cases potentially fatal) symptoms while the addict's system readjusts to the absence of the drug in question.

Challenges for society

Drug addiction takes a terrible toll on both addicts and those around them, and is a huge challenge for society at large: as well as countless deaths from drug overdoses each year, countries around the world struggle (and in many cases fail entirely) to cope with the impact of addiction on individuals' physical and mental health.

Huge levels of crime are associated with drug abuse and addiction. From individual cases of theft or prostitution right the way through to the multibillion-dollar drug-trafficking market and the catastrophic levels of violence with which drug abuse goes hand-in-hand.

Some countries are effectively in the middle of civil wars as a result of the depth to which drug cartels have penetrated the social fabric, while even in less dramatic circumstances street-level violence is an inescapable corollary to the supply and consumption of illegal drugs.

The difference between abuse and addiction

Drug abuse is not the same as drug addiction: it is possible to abuse drugs without being addicted to them. Drug abuse occurs when someone consumes a drug in quantities or via methods which can harm themselves or other people – but this does not necessarily imply the compulsive, repeated consumption of the drug which indicates addiction.

Drug abuse can occur as a one-off – someone may abuse a given drug and then never take it again – or can take place repeatedly – even frequently – without addiction developing; however, the more frequently a person indulges in drug abuse, the more likely it is that they will develop an addiction to that drug.

Both drug abuse and addiction can have hugely deleterious consequences for the person consuming the drug or drugs: just because someone isn't addicted to a drug does not mean that they are safe from overdose (indeed each year a tragically high number of people die worldwide from taking drugs for the first time), nor from the legal consequences of drug possession.

Certainly, there is a greatly increased probability that they will become involved in an accident or participate in risky behaviour which may have catastrophic long-term consequences. Moreover, even if someone is not actually addicted to a drug, long-term drug abuse can have long-lasting or even permanent consequences for their physical and mental health.

Complications and consequences

Drug addiction tends to have a number of consequences which may not apply to drug abuse in all circumstances – for example, although drug abuse can be costly, drug addiction typically implies a very significant long-term financial commitment from which it is very hard to escape without help, whereas someone abusing drugs who is not, however, addicted to them may stop taking them at any point at will and avoid those potentially devastating costs.

Similarly, if someone abusing drugs begins to experience negative impacts upon their self-esteem and/or hopes for the future as a result, they can stop that abuse and immediately avoid those impacts; an addict, however, is imprisoned by their addiction and cannot escape those negative emotional consequences, which understandably can lead to serious mental health issues including depression.

What causes drug addiction?

Although drug addiction has been a problem for many thousands of years – in the case of alcoholism, especially, it is likely to have been a phenomenon which emerged in prehistoric times – we are still not entirely certain about what exactly causes it, but both genetic and environmental factors can play a role.

Genetics

Some people are genetically more predisposed than others to developing addictions, while a host of environmental risk factors – for example an exposure to substances of abuse in childhood, or experiencing trauma either in childhood or later in life – are recognised as greatly increasing the likelihood that a person will struggle with addiction at some point or other in their life.

However, while one person may be exposed to an array of these risk factors and develop a drug addiction, another may experience the same risk factors (perhaps as a member of the same family, even a sibling – and therefore also with a similar genetic makeup) and yet remain addiction-free their whole life.

Some studies of alcoholism specifically indicate that genetic factors account for around half of the risk factors for that condition, and some scientists have found similar rates of heritability for addiction to other substances.

A number of specific genes have been identified as being associated with a greater risk of addiction, but their precise role remains as yet unclear and most scientists believe that there exist many other genes which also play a role but which have yet to be identified and/or their relationship with addiction has not yet been proven.

Environment

Meanwhile, scientists and psychologists have identified certain environmental factors which are more prominent than others in terms of their impact on a person's overall predisposition towards addiction.

Childhood abuse and/or dysfunctional family environment during childhood and adolescence, the prevalence of substance abuse amongst a young person's peers, poverty, and witnessing or experiencing traumatic events all greatly increase the likelihood that someone will develop an addiction.

However, it is possible that a person can be exposed to all of those risk factors and more and yet never become addicted to any substance of abuse – and on the other hand, it is also possible that someone can have none of those risk factors associated with them and yet turn out to be an addict. Put simply, there is no one hard and fast "recipe" for addiction which scientists and the medical community have yet been able to identify with certainty.

Of course, there is one factor above all which drives addiction: the repeated consumption of an addictive substance. It is possible, unfortunately, that even someone with no predisposition towards addiction can become an addict through repeated drug consumption.

Some medicines are habit-forming (indeed, some of the most dangerous substances in terms of the risks posed by their withdrawal symptoms are prescription drugs, namely benzodiazepines) and a lamentably high number of addicts today first became addicted through prolonged and repeated consumption of medication (for example, opioids to treat chronic pain).

Indeed, many people who would never dream of touching a substance of abuse, let alone indulge in repeated drug abuse at a frequency likely to result in addiction, become "accidentally" addicted in this manner.

Sadly, many people addicted to strong and dangerous illegal drugs such as heroin first developed their addictions in hospital whilst being delivered pain-relieving medicine such as morphine, and found themselves unable to stop consuming such drugs once their treatment and/or time in hospital was concluded, thus being driven to procure illegal drugs on the street.

Who is most likely to become a drug addict?

It is impossible to say for sure who will and will not become an addict. Moreover, because of the aforementioned possibility of becoming addicted inadvertently and without initially engaging in recreational drug use and abuse, it is theoretically possible for absolutely anybody to become a drug addict.

However, there are certain types of people who are at a higher risk than others of developing drug addiction. One important factor is the age at which a person begins abusing drugs: put simply, the younger the person is when they first consume a substance of abuse, the greater the likelihood that they will develop an addiction at some point in their life.

This is not, it must be stressed, a hard and fast rule in that it is very possible for someone to consume drugs at a very young age and not become addicted at any point (so parents of children found consuming drugs need not sink into despair believing that their children are now doomed inescapably to addiction); nevertheless the correlation is a strong one.

Similarly strong is the correlation between survivors of abuse and drug addiction: one landmark study put the chance of someone developing addiction who has experienced at least five traumatic events at 4,600% greater than that of someone who has not experienced any trauma.

Furthermore, this goes some way to explain why people in certain professions who are more likely to be exposed to traumatic events – for example soldiers or emergency responders – are also more likely to develop addictions at some point.

There is also a very strong correlation between mental health issues and substance abuse and addiction: people suffering from serious mental disorders are much more likely than the average to go on to develop addictions, in part because they are quite likely to self-medicate with substances of abuse.

The link between depression and substance abuse (which tends to be a vicious circle, as substance abuse itself can cause and/or exacerbate depression) is well known; less well understood, but increasingly the subject of clinical research, is the connection between autism and similar conditions and addiction.

Understandably, anyone suffering from chronic pain has a greatly increased likelihood of developing addiction as a result of their consumption of pain-relieving medications, many of which as noted are extremely addictive. Interestingly, it is also the case that people with access to such medications who do not however necessarily require them themselves – for example, doctors and nurses – are also more likely than the average person to become addicted at some time in their lives.

The bottom line, effectively, is that anybody can become addicted who regularly takes an addictive substance, for whatever reason. While the types of person mentioned above are statistically more likely than the average to become addicted to a substance of abuse at some point.

That does not mean that someone who does not fall into any of the above categories is unlikely to suffer from addiction if they consume addictive substances with any regularity – and nor does it mean that someone who does fit into one of those categories will inevitably develop an addiction. Just as every person is unique, so is every case of addiction and the circumstances surrounding it.

5 September 2018

The above information is reprinted with kind permission from UK Addiction Treatment Centres.

www.ukat.co.uk

Acid (LSD) and magic mushrooms (shrooms)

Short term: Acid and magic mushrooms are hallucinogenics, making people see, hear and experience the world in a different, "trippy" way. Colours may become intensified and sounds distorted.

Users may also become panicky and suffer from paranoia.

The effects of acid can last 12 hours or more which, if it's a bad trip, can be very frightening.

Long term: Some people who use LSD and magic mushrooms can experience flashbacks. Both can make existing mental health problems worse.

Anabolic steroids (roids)

Short term: Anabolic steroids pump up muscle mass but can also make you feel paranoid, irritable, aggressive or even violent (what's known as "roid rage").

Long term: People can become psychologically dependent on anabolic steroids, and convinced they cannot perform well without them.

Cannabis (marijuana, weed, dope, skunk)

Short term: People smoke cannabis to relax and get high, but it can make it difficult to remember things. It can also cause anxiety attacks or feelings of paranoia.

Long term: Cannabis may trigger long-term mental health problems, including psychosis.

Cannabis users who have a family history of mental health problems and who start using it in their teens are particularly at risk.

About 10% of regular cannabis users become addicted to it.

Cocaine and crack cocaine

Short term: Cocaine comes in three forms:

- powder
- freebase (where the powder is prepared for smoking)
- crack ("rocks" of cocaine that are smoked)

Cocaine is a stimulant that makes you feel high, confident and full of energy. But this can turn into feelings of anxiety, panic and paranoia.

Regular cocaine users can end up feeling exhausted and depressed.

Long term: Cocaine is addictive. Giving it up can be mentally distressing and physically difficult.

Long-term use can make existing mental health problems worse and lead to depression, anxiety and paranoia.

Ecstasy (E)

Short term: Ecstasy is a stimulant with hallucinogenic effects that makes you feel relaxed, high, "loved-up" and ready to dance all night.

But people who are already feeling anxious or who take high doses can experience paranoia or panic attacks.

Long term: Regular use may lead to lack of energy, memory loss, anxiety and depression.

Heroin (smack, diamorphine)

Short term: Heroin and other opiates slow down the body and stop both physical and emotional pain.

People find they need to take more and more heroin to get the same effect, or even feel "normal". Taking a lot can lead to coma or even death.

Long term: Heroin is psychologically and physically highly addictive. Withdrawal from heroin is unpleasant, and coming off and staying off it can be very difficult.

Long-term heroin users may be depressed because of their overall lifestyle.

Ketamine (K)

Short term: Ketamine is an anaesthetic that makes people feel relaxed and high, but its effects are unpredictable.

You may not be aware of what you are doing after taking it so you risk, for example, having an accident.

Long term: The longer term effects may include flashbacks, losing your memory and not being able to concentrate.

Regular use can cause depression and, occasionally, psychotic symptoms such as hallucinations.

Ketamine can also make existing mental health problems worse.

Solvents (gases, glues and aerosols)

Short term: Solvents make you feel high and disorientated. They can cause aggression, mood swings and hallucinations.

Long term: Heavy use of solvents can damage your brain, particularly the bit that controls your movements.

Speed and crystal meth (amphetamine and methamphetamine)

Short term: Speed can make you feel energetic and confident but it can also cause anxiety, paranoia and aggression.

The "comedown" can make you feel lethargic and down, and you may have problems with concentrating and learning.

The effects of crystal meth are similar to speed but more exaggerated and longer-lasting. The comedown can be worse too.

Long term: Heavy use of speed can lead to anxiety, depression, irritability, aggression and paranoia. It can also cause psychotic symptoms, such as hallucinations.

Regular use of crystal meth can lead to brain damage, but this can be reversed if you don't use the drug for a long time.

Tranquillisers (benzodiazepines)

Short term: Tranquillisers, such as diazepam, are sedative drugs. They are used to treat anxiety and aid sleep.

Big doses of tranquillisers can affect your memory and make you drowsy.

Long term: Your body quickly gets used to benzodiazepines and soon needs more to get the same effect. You can get addicted in just a few weeks. Withdrawal can be difficult and make you feel panicky, anxious and depressed.

Sudden withdrawal from high doses can be very dangerous and cause seizures (fits).

18 February 2020

Statistics on drug misuse, England 2019

An extract from Hospital admissions related to drug misuse from an Office for National Statistics publication

Key facts

Key facts cover the latest year of data available:

- Hospital admissions – 2018/19
- Deaths (England & Wales) – 2018
- Adult drug use (England & Wales) – 2018/19

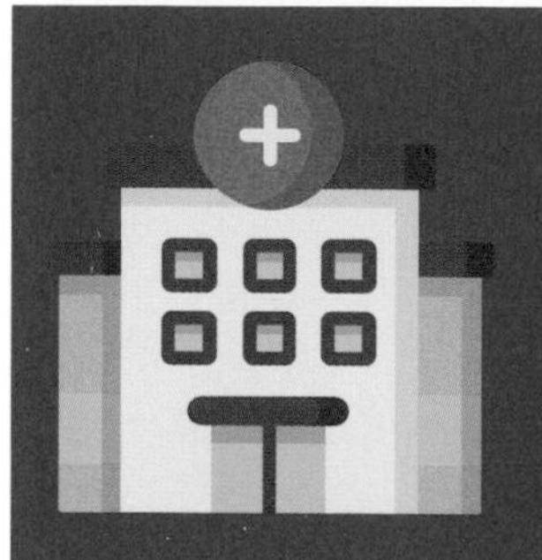

7,376 hospital admissions for drug related mental and behavioural disorders

14 % less than 3 years ago in 2015/16 (8,621), but still 30% higher than in 2008/09 (5,668)

Admissions were around 6 times more likely in the most deprived areas compared to the least deprived areas

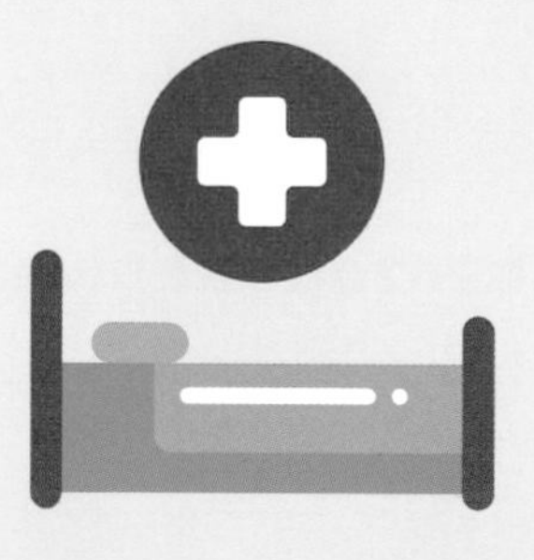

18,053 hospital admissions for poisoning by drug misuse

A 6% increase on 2017/18, and 16% higher than in 2012/13 (15,580)

Admissions were around 5 times more likely in the most deprived areas compared to the least deprived areas

2,917 deaths related to poisoning by drug misuse

A 17% increase on 2017 (2,503), and 46% higher than ten years ago in 2008 (2,004)

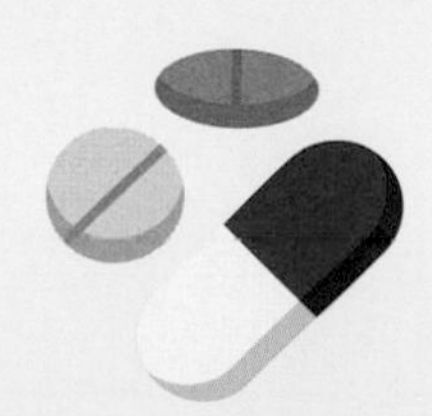

9.4% adults (16 to 59) had taken an illicit drug in the last year

20.3% of young adults (16-24) had teaken an illicit drug in the last year

Admissions by sex

More men than women were admitted to hospital for drug related mental and behavioural disorders (74% male), but similar proportions for admissions due to poisoning by drug misuse

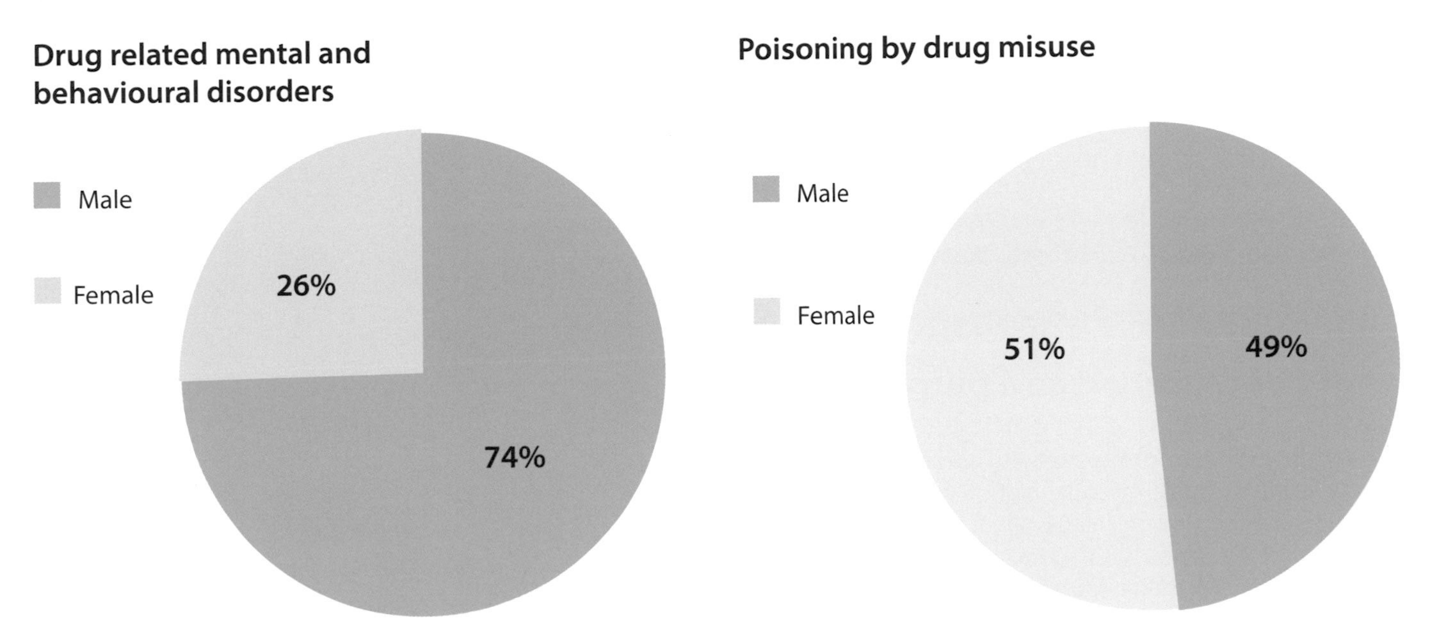

Admissions by age

Admissions for drug related mental and behavioural disorders, and for poisoning by drug misuse, showed similar age profiles. Levels were highest for younger people (apart from those under 16), peaking between ages 25 and 34. Admissions for drug related mental and behavioural disorders are very uncommon in those aged under 16 and over 64.

For drug related mental and behavioural disorders

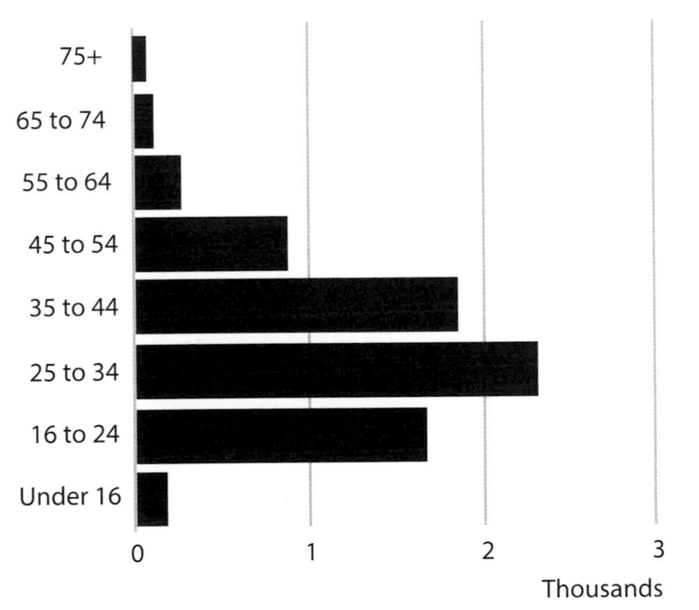

For poisoning by drug use

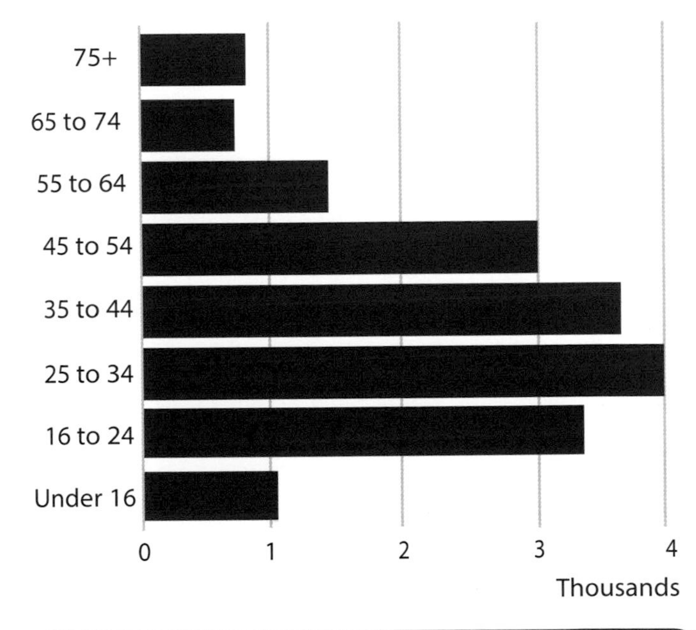

www.digital.nhs.uk

Scottish Schools Adolescent Lifestyle and Substance Use Survey (SALSUS): drug use report 2018

Findings on drug use from the 2018 wave of the Scottish Schools Adolescent Lifestyle and Substance Use Survey (SALSUS).

Introduction

This report presents the drug use findings from the 2018 wave of the Scottish Schools Adolescent Lifestyle and Substance Use Survey (SALSUS). The research was commissioned by the Scottish Government and carried out by Ipsos MORI Scotland.

Survey background and purpose

SALSUS is a continuation of a long established series of national surveys on smoking, drinking and drug use. These were carried out jointly in Scotland and England between 1982 and 2000, to provide a national picture of young people's smoking (from 1982), drinking (from 1990), and drug use (from 1998) behaviours within the context of other lifestyle, health and social factors. Since 2002, Scotland has developed its own, more tailored survey, known as SALSUS.

About the survey

SALSUS is a self-completion survey administered by teachers in a mixed ability class, under exam conditions. In 2018, schools were encouraged to administer the survey online (but could administer it on paper if that was more feasible). Fieldwork was undertaken between September 2018 and April 2019.

The overall response rate was 52% based on class and pupil response rate.

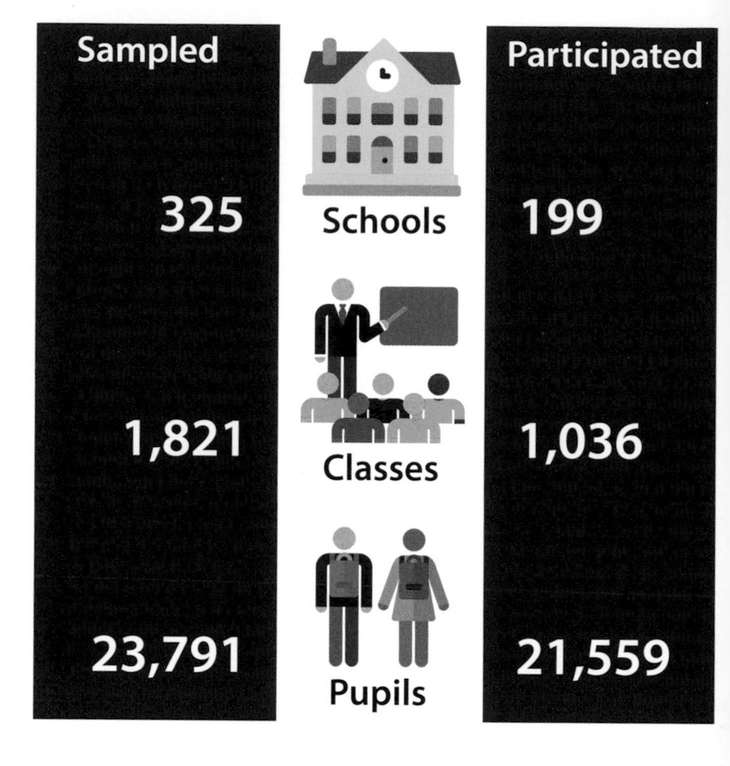

Key findings

Prevalence and key trends

- 6% of 13 year olds and 21% of 15 year olds had ever used drugs.
- 4% of 13 year olds and 12% of 15 year olds reported using drugs in the last month.
- Drug use in the last month has been gradually decreasing since 2002, when 8% of 13 year olds and 23% of 15 year olds reported using drugs in the last month. However, between 2013 and 2018, there was an increase in the proportion of 13 year old and 15 year old boys who took drugs in the month prior to the survey (from 2% and 11% respectively in 2013, to 4% and 15% in 2018).
- Cannabis was the most widely used drug; 19% of 15 year olds had ever used cannabis.
- 6% of 15 year olds had ever taken ecstasy, 5% had ever taken cocaine, 5% had ever taken any form of Novel Psychoactive Substances (NPS) and 5% had ever taken MDMA powder.
- 31% of 13 year olds and 42% of 15 year olds who had ever used drugs had been drinking alcohol the last time they had used drugs. 15% of all pupils had used more than one drug (polydrug use) the last time they had used drugs
- 36% of 13 year olds and 45% of 15 year olds who had ever taken drugs had experienced at least one negative effect as a result (in the last year). The most common effects were having an argument, vomiting, and doing something they later regretted.
- It was most common for pupils to have used drugs out in the street or in someone else's home.

Sources and availability

- 22% of 13 year olds and 47% of 15 year olds had ever been offered drugs. There was an increase in the proportion who had ever been offered drugs between 2015 and 2018 (from 19% to 22% among 13 year olds and from 42% to 47% among 15 year olds).
- 15 year old pupils were most commonly offered cannabis. 37% of all 15 year olds had been offered cannabis, 18% had been offered ecstasy, 15% had been offered cocaine, and 14% had been offered MDMA powder or some form of NPS.
- Since 2015, there has been an increase in the proportions of 15 year olds who have been offered cannabis, cocaine, MDMA powder, LSD and ketamine.
- It was most common for pupils who had ever taken drugs to get them from friends (friends of the same age or older).

Attitudes to drugs

- Among 15 year olds, the acceptability of trying cannabis and sniffing glue has increased since 2015 – 33% of 15 year olds thought it was 'ok' to try cannabis, compared with 24% in 2015, and 11% thought it was 'ok' to try sniffing glue, compared with 7% in 2015.
- 9% of 15 year olds thought it was 'ok' to try cocaine.

26 November 2019

Drug-related deaths in Scotland in 2018

Drug-related deaths 2018

Summary

Drug-related deaths continue to increase

The number of drug-related deaths increased by 27% in 2018 to reach 1,187 - the largest number ever recorded and more than double the number recorded a decade ago.

The shaded area shows the likely range of variation around the 5-year moving average

Largest increases in 35-54 year olds

Most of the increase in drug-related death rates has occurred in the 35-44 year old and 45-54 year old age groups.

*Rates per 1,000 population

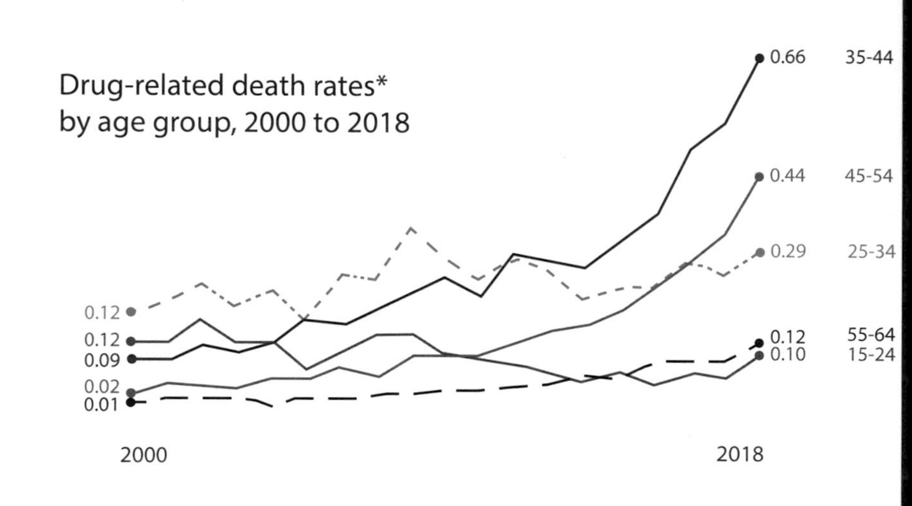

Death rates vary geographically

Greater Glasgow & Clyde had the highest rate at 0.23 per 1,000 population, followed by Tayside and Ayrshire & Arran with rates of 0.18 and 0.17 per 1,000 population respectively.

*Rates are based on 5-year averages to reduce year-to-year fluctuations.

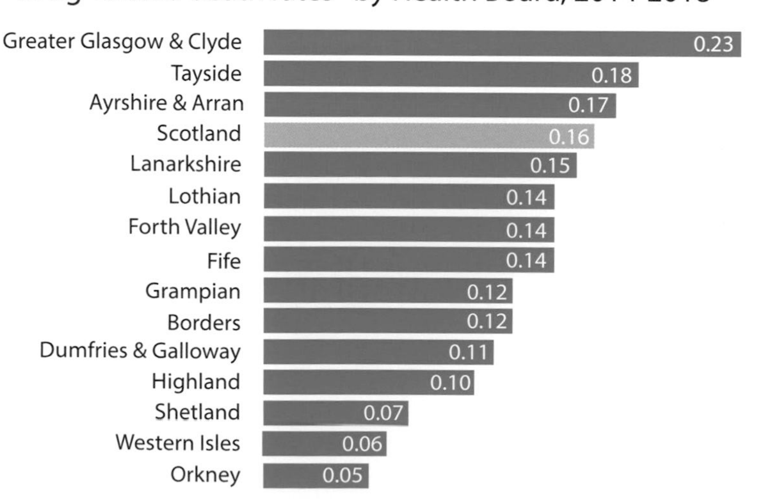

Scotland has worst drugs problem in Europe as death rate soars

More than 1,000 deaths involved methadone, heroin and morphine, but a large percentage of those who died - 792 - had also taken pills such as diazepam.

By Auslan Cramb

Scotland's drugs death rate is now higher than the USA and every other country in Europe, and three times the UK average, according to shocking new figures.

The statistics released on Tuesday revealed that 1,187 people died following drug use last year, an increase of 27 per cent on 2017.

Methadone, the heroin substitute prescribed by the NHS to help heroin users, caused more deaths than the drug it is meant to replace and contributed to nearly half the total mortality figure.

The National Records of Scotland said the country now had a higher mortality rate than any other country in Europe.

In the US, the latest figures suggest a drug death rate of 217 per million people, compared to a figure in Scotland of 218 per million.

The Scottish total is at the highest level since current records began in 1996 and is more than double the 2008 figure of 574.

The statistics show that 72 per cent of those who died were male, with more than 1,000 deaths involving methadone, heroin and morphine. However, a large percentage of those who died - 792 - had also taken pills such as diazepam and etizolam.

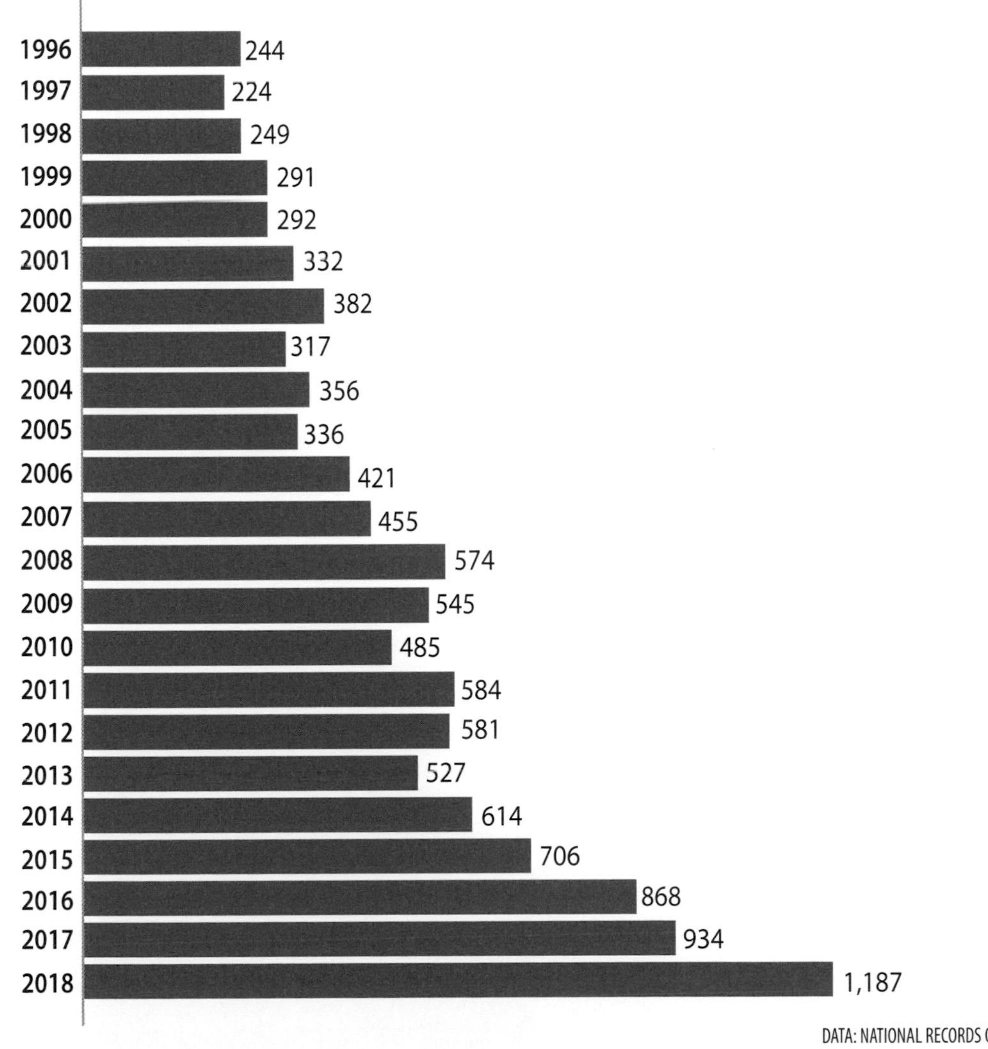

It was reported last month that these “street valiums” can be bought for less than the price of a chocolate bar, at just 30p a pill in central Glasgow, and are often taken in conjunction with opiates, with fatal consequences.

Scotland’s Public Health Minister Joe FitzPatrick said the figures were “shocking”, and bold new approaches were needed to save lives. He also repeated calls for the UK Government to enable the creation of safer “drug consumption rooms”.

But the Scottish Conservatives said SNP administration had presided over the catastrophic rise in drug deaths after having sole control over health and justice for the past 12 years.

Annie Wells, Conservative public health spokesperson, said the crisis should be the number one concern for Nicola Sturgeon and the Scottish Government.

She added: 'On its watch, these fatalities – all of which are avoidable – have more than doubled since it came to power.

'The SNP has had control over health and justice for 12 years, yet hasn’t managed to bring in anything that comes close to dealing with this problem.

'As these figures show, whatever drugs strategies it has adopted have only made things worse.

'Predictably, in their desperation, the nationalists are now pinning their hopes on consumption rooms, because they know it’s something the UK Government does not agree with.

'That’s a cowardly approach from those ministers who’re meant to be taking responsibility. Instead, they’re hiding behind a ruse.'

The Tories called for a strategy based on rehabilitation and "abstinence-based recovery", services which they said had been cut by the SNP.

Ms Wells added: 'Over the last decade, the Scottish Government’s approach has been to park vulnerable users on methadone. Yet these figures show methadone now causes even more deaths than heroin.'

Miles Briggs, the shadow health secretary, said drug and alcohol partnerships were the “Cinderella” service of the NHS and the figures were an indictment of 20 years of failed drug policies under Labour, Lib Dem and SNP governments.

He called for a review of the methadone programme and new fast-track residential rehabilitation places.

He added: 'SNP ministers have taken the regressive decisions to cut alcohol and drug partnership budgets in the past which has resulted in the destabilisation of services across the country.'

Greater Glasgow & Clyde had the highest rate at 0.23 per 1,000 population, followed by Tayside and Ayrshire & Arran with rates of 0.18 and 0.17 per 1,000 population respectively.

16 July 2019

Millions of people in England taking medicines they can find hard to stop

NHS must take action to avoid US-style opioid crisis, says co-author of government study.

By Sarah Bosley, Health editor

Nearly 12 million people – about one in four adults in England – are taking medicines for pain, depression or insomnia, which they can find hard to stop, according to a government review.

Too many people are being prescribed medicines that can cause dependence, says Public Health England (PHE). Half have been on these medicines for a year or more and more than a fifth for over three years. Prescribing rates are 1.5 times higher for women than for men.

There may be good reasons for people to use antidepressants over a long period, but the widespread prescribing of opioid painkillers, benzodiazepines and sleeping pills needs to change, the review says. GPs should instead consider social prescribing, from talking therapies to joining a choir.

The biggest numbers are on antidepressants, which are taken by 7.3 million people in England, or 17% of the adult population. About 930,000 people have been on them for at least three years. Those who stop need to do so with the help of a doctor and taper their dose gradually to avoid withdrawal symptoms.

But long-term antidepressant use is necessary for some. More worrying, say the experts, are the half a million people who have been on opioid painkillers for more than three years for chronic conditions such as lower back pain and joint pain. The drugs are addictive and paracetamol or ibuprofen work as well or better, say experts. Opioids should be kept for acute pain, such as in cancer.

The review looked at five categories of drugs – antidepressants, opioid painkillers, benzodiazepines mostly prescribed for anxiety, gabapentinoids for neuropathic pain and z-drugs for insomnia. Prescribing of both opioids and benzodiazepines is dropping, but only after rising for many years.

Peter Burkinshaw at PHE, one of the authors, said: 'The long-term prescribing of opioid pain medicines and benzodiazepines is not supported by guidelines and is not effective.'

They found poorer people were more likely to be at risk of long-term prescription and more people were on the medicines for protracted periods in the north-east and north-west of the country, Burkinshaw said. 'Prescribing rates are higher and duration is longer in areas of deprivation in England,' he said.

Fellow author Rosanna O'Connor, said: "We know that GPs in some of the more deprived areas are under great pressure but, as this review highlights, more needs to be done to educate and support patients, as well as looking closely at prescribing practice and what alternative treatments are available locally.

'While the scale and nature of opioid prescribing does not reflect the so-called crisis in North America, the NHS needs to take action now to protect patients.'

PHE officials urged people who were taking these medicines not to stop them abruptly, but if they were worried to speak to their GP.

Prof Helen Stokes-Lampard, the chair of the Royal College of GPs, said family doctors needed better access to alternatives to drug treatment. Most prescriptions were short-term and opioids were on the decline, but the review showed 'the severe lack of alternatives to drug therapies for many conditions – and where effective alternatives are known and exist, inadequate and unequal access to them across the country', she said.

GPs did not want to put patients on long-term medication, but for some it was the only thing that helped with distressing conditions such as chronic pain, depression and anxiety, she said.

The report recommends new guidance for GPs and better information for patients on the risks and benefits of the medicines, as well as improved data collection and a national helpline for worried members of the public. The National Institute for Health and Care Excellence said it was working on a guideline for the NHS on the safe prescribing and withdrawal of prescribed drugs.

The Royal College of Psychiatrists welcomed the report. 'The findings of this review must be carefully listened to,' said Prof Wendy Burn, its president. "These drugs are important to the health and wellbeing of many patients when prescribed properly, but guidance for doctors needs to be updated to reflect the experience of patients who experience negative effects of withdrawal.'

'Antidepressants can bring significant benefits to many people's lives. In all treatments, medicines which do good can also have negative effects. As the review acknowledges, long-term antidepressant use can be entirely clinically appropriate. However, patients must be supported to come off any prescription medication if they choose to and it is safe for them to do this.'

Prof John Read from the University of East London, who represented the British Psychological Society on the PHE inquiry and was joint author of an influential review for MPs on the withdrawal problems with antidepressants, said this was a hugely important report.

'We especially welcome the thorough research review documenting the alarming numbers of people experiencing withdrawal effects from prescribed medicines, and the recommendations for urgently needed services and a phone line to support people struggling to come off these drugs, including antidepressants,' he said.

'We also value the emphasis placed on increasing accessibility to talking therapies for the problems that the drugs are currently prescribed for.'

10 September 2019

www.theguardian.com

Baby boomers are increasingly more likely to risk drink driving than millennials

An article from The Conversation.

THE CONVERSATION

By Tony Rao, Visiting Lecturer in Old Age Psychiatry, King's College London

"Baby boomers", all now over the age of 50, have shown the fastest rise in rates of alcohol and drug misuse over the past 15 years – and this is playing out on Britain's roads.

At first glance, the latest data on reported accidents and casualties on public roads in England and Wales is little more than a general update. There are the standard statistics on drink drive accidents and casualties using roadside breath testing. There is also data on blood alcohol levels for accidents involving deaths from drink driving. In 2017, there were just under 171,000 casualties from reported road traffic accidents. This was 6% lower than in 2016 – making it the lowest level on record.

But more revealing data comes from the British Crime Survey. The Survey looked at self-reported driving by people who

think that they have been over the legal alcohol limit at least once in the last 12 months. Between 2010 and 2018, there was a reduction of nearly 50% in the proportion of people aged 16 to 19 who took this risk. For people aged 50, it fell by only 11%.

The same survey also provided data on the proportion of people reporting driving under the influence of drugs over the previous 12 months – which paints a very different picture. Although there was a reduction of 61% for 16- to 19 year-olds over the past ten years, the reduction for baby boomers was a staggering 98%.

A likely explanation for the comparatively larger reductions in people willing to take the risk of drug driving compared with drink driving may be a change in the law over the past four years. Until 2015, there were no defined limits for individual controlled drugs when bringing charges against someone suspected of drug driving. This changed in 2015 through the introduction of Section 5A of the Road Traffic Act. This set an upper limit for the level of specific controlled drugs in a driver's blood.

A report assessing the impact of this change in law enforcement found evidence of an improvement in awareness of the change in law enforcement among road users across all age groups. This appears to have been an even bigger deterrent to drug driving in older people.

Cultural norms

So why then are older drivers more prepared to risk drink driving than drug driving? Part of this may be the influence of cultural norms, such as being exposed to high levels of advertising during their early years, but also to the increased affordability of alcohol.

An upper legal limit of 80 milligrammes of alcohol per 100ml (also referred to as 0.08%) of blood was adopted across Europe over 50 years ago. Unlike the rest of Europe and Scotland, the rest of the UK has not changed this legal level. In Scotland, for example it is now 0.05%

In 2013, the National Transportation Safety Board in the US reduced the legal limit for blood alcohol from 0.08% to 0.05%. This resulted in an 11% decline in fatal alcohol-related crashes.

Slow reactions

Even without drinking alcohol, older people have slower reaction times and are less able to maintain a constant distance behind another car during driving simulation compared to younger people.

Older people are also more likely to experience the harmful effects of alcohol after drinking the same quantity of alcohol as younger people. This is because of a reduced ability to remove alcohol from the bloodstream, as well as a higher likelihood of taking prescribed medication and having accompanying long-term health problems.

So should there be a lower legal blood alcohol level? Given that baby boomers are at increasingly higher risk of alcohol misuse and are more likely to take the risk of drink driving compared with drug driving, it may be the only direction of travel. After all, alcohol is a drug. And the sooner it's treated like one, the better.

14 March 2019

Vaping deaths: Are e-cigarettes really safer than smoking tobacco? A complete guide to the facts

By Emma Snaith

1. Is vaping better than smoking?

2. What are the health risks attached?

3. Who has died from vaping?

4. Why did the CEO of Juul step down?

5 Which countries have banned vaping?

Vaping has been heralded as a healthier alternative to smoking cigarettes, but what do you need to know about the risks attached?

In the US an outbreak of vaping-related illnesses has been linked to 39 deaths and 2,000 cases of lung injury, according to the Centers for Disease Control and Prevention.

Donald Trump is now considering plans to ban all flavoured e-cigarette products following the spike in lung illnesses. Health chiefs in the US are warning people to avoid vaping completely until the cause of the deaths is clear.

It is thought that Vitamin E acetate, an oily chemical added to some THC vaping liquids, could be behind the mystery illness after the substance was found in every lung fluid sample from afflicted patients.

But in the UK, no vaping-related deaths have been confirmed and health officials continue to endorse e-cigarettes as an effective way to quit smoking.

Meanwhile, a number of countries including India, Brazil and Thailand have banned e-cigarettes over growing health concerns. Yet the number of adults who vape around the world is expected to reach almost 55m by 2021, according to market research group Euromonitor.

1. Is vaping better than smoking?

E-cigarettes, also known as vapourisers or vapes, allow users to inhale nicotine in vapour rather than breathing in smoke. Unlike cigarettes, they do not burn tobacco or produce tar or carbon monoxide. However, they do contain nicotine, which is addictive but relatively harmless.

Vaping is far less harmful than smoking, experts from a number of key bodies including Cancer Research UK, Public Health England and the US National Academies of Sciences, Engineering and Medicine have concluded.

Both the NHS and Public Health England (PHE) support the use of vaping over smoking. In 2015, a report from PHE estimated vaping was 95 per cent less harmful than smoking.

Ann McNeill, professor of Tobacco Addiction at King's College London, told The Independent: "Vaping isn't risk free, but it's much less risky than smoking, which kills nearly 100,000 people a year in the UK.

'If you are a smoker who is struggling to stop smoking, do try vaping and buy your products from a reputable source. And if you are a vaper, it is better to continue to vape than relapse to smoking.'

Professor John Newton, director for health improvement at PHE, said: 'Vaping is not without risks. If you don't smoke don't vape.

'But if you smoke there is no situation where it would be better for your health to continue smoking rather than switching completely to vaping. The sooner you stop smoking completely the better.'

Cigarette smoking is the leading preventable cause of death in the US, according to the Centers for Disease Control. It kills 480,000 people each year, nearly one in five deaths.

Tobacco is also one of the major causes of death and disease in India, accounting for nearly 900,000 deaths every year. In the UK it causes nearly 80,000 deaths a year.

A major UK National Institute Health Research funded clinical trial found e-cigarettes were almost twice as effective at helping smokers to quit compared with other alternatives such as nicotine patches and gum.

2. What are the health risks attached?

Experts estimate 20,000 smokers who take up e-cigarettes are quitting smoking each year in the UK alone.

But vaping is not without its risks.

More than 805 cases of lung disease and 12 deaths in the US have been linked to vaping, according to the Centre for Disease Control (CDC).

While the CDC is investigating the causes of this outbreak, they have advised people to avoid using vaping products, particularly those containing cannabis products.

In the UK, vaping has been linked to 200 health problems including pneumonia and heart disorders over the last five years, according to the Medicines and Healthcare Regulatory Agency (MHRA).

The MHRA said it is reviewing the information gathered in 74 separate 'Yellow Card' reports filed by the public and healthcare professionals. But the watchdog emphasises the reports are not proof the adverse effects were due to e-cigarettes, but a suspicion by people reporting ailments that the device is to blame.

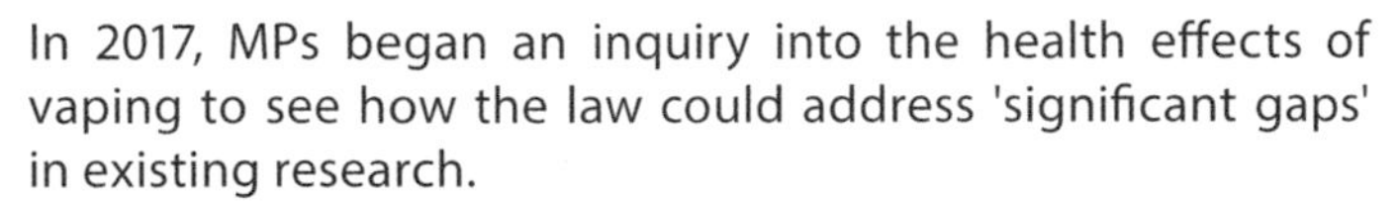

In 2017, MPs began an inquiry into the health effects of vaping to see how the law could address 'significant gaps' in existing research.

It has gone on to note 'there is clear evidence that e-cigarettes are substantially less harmful than conventional cigarettes'. It added 'there are uncertainties, nevertheless, especially about any long-term health effects of e-cigarettes, because the products have not yet had a history of long use'.

Public Health England (PHE) said most of the American cases of vaping-related illnesses were linked to people using "illicit vaping fluid' bought on the streets or containing cannabis products.

Deborah Arnott, the chief executive of anti-smoking charity Action on Smoking Health (ASH), told The Independent vapers in the UK 'should not be scared back to smoking by the news of vaping illness in the US'.

'Nor should smokers stick to smoking rather than switch to vaping,' she added. 'It is essential, however, to only use legal vapes bought from reputable suppliers in the UK and not source illicit unregulated products over the internet.'

There is limited evidence to suggest vaping causes harm to other people around you. According to the NHS, 'the available evidence indicates that any risk of harm is extremely low, especially when compared with second-hand tobacco smoke'.

3. Who has died from vaping?

An outbreak of vaping-related deaths in the US has been described as a public health crisis.

At least 39 people have died and more than 2,000 have suffered lung injuries from vaping-related illnesses, according to the Centers for Disease Control and Prevention (CDC).

Currently 46 states and one US territory have reported cases of the illness. Two thirds of those with the illness are 18 to 34-years-old, while 16 per cent are under 18. Around 69 per cent of the patients are male.

Most patients have reported a history of using products containing THC, the psychoactive compound in cannabis. But one patient who died in Georgia last month reported only 'heavy nicotine vaping'.

Health researchers believe vitamin E acetate, a chemical added to some THC vaping liquids, could be behind the mystery illness. The substance was found in every lung fluid sample from afflicted patients tested by the CDC.

A man in Texas was also killed after an e-cigarette he used exploded in his face and tore his carotid artery causing a massive stroke.

There have been no confirmed deaths linked to vaping in the UK.

However, some doctors believe the death of 57-year-old British factory worker Terry Miller from lipoid pneumonia was linked to vaping after oil from an e-cigarette was found in his lungs. A coroner returned an open verdict at the inquest after saying he could not be sure whether vaping was a contributory factor.

Last year after a 34-year-old woman developed lipoid pneumonia, doctors identified the cause as vegetable glycerine found in e-cigarettes, according to a case report in the British Medical Journal.

But the link between vaping and lipoid pneumonia is disputed. Ann McNeill, professor of Tobacco Addiction at King's College London, told The Independent that in the case of the 34-year-old woman it "doesn't really add up" that her illness was caused by vaping a nicotine e-cigarette.

"The case of lipoid pneumonia was allegedly caused by glycerin in the vape liquid the patient was inhaling - but glycerin is water soluble and an alcohol and not a lipid," she said. "So the glycerin is unlikely to cause lipoid pneumonia."

4. Why did the CEO of Juul step down?

Amid the sudden surge of vaping-related deaths and illnesses in the US, the CEO of tobacco vaping company Juul stepped down in September.

It came after a 17-year-old who said vaping gave him lungs "like a 70-year-old" announced he was suing the company for marketing e-cigarettes to young people.

Former CEO Kevin Burns had previously warned non-smokers against using Juul products, stating they were not the firm's "target consumer".

After launching in 2015, Juul emerged as the largest e-cigarette brand in the US two years later.

In hundreds of lawsuits filed in federal and local courts across the US, lawyers blame Juul for the rise in youth vaping. They accuse the company of a targeted marketing campaign directed at young adults.

Just over 20 per cent of US middle and high school students were found to use e-cigarettes in 2018, according to the US surgeon general. This was an increase of 78 per cent from the previous year. Between 2011-2015 e-cigarette use increased by 900 per cent among this age group.

In the UK, 15 per cent of 11-18 year-olds tried vaping in 2019 compared to 16 per cent in the previous year, according to a study conducted by anti-smoking charity Action on Smoking Health. But there was an increase in the number of current vapers in that age group from 5 per cent in 2019 compared to 3 per cent in 2018.

Among those surveyed, Juul had the highest brand awareness among 11-18 year-olds but only 7 per cent were able to name it unprompted.

5. Which countries have banned vaping?

Governments around the world are divided about vaping. Thirty-nine countries have banned the sale of e-cigarettes or nicotine liquids, according to the 2018 Global State of Tobacco Harm Reduction report.

In the US, Donald Trump said he planned to ban flavoured e-cigarettes in September following a spate of vaping-related deaths. The Food and Drug Administration will develop guidelines to remove from the market all e-cigarette flavours except tobacco.

12 November 2019

What is vaping and is it safe?

Vaping has exploded in popularity with young people. But the case against e-cigarettes — for smokers and non-smokers — is mounting.

By Maggie Fox

Vaping can sound so pleasant — a small device that you can use to inhale fruit or candy-flavoured water vapour. It's the 21st century answer to smoking: it doesn't make your breath smell, it's discreet and it's so much safer than smoking tobacco.

Or is it?

There's a debate over whether e-cigarettes should be more strongly regulated. The U.S. federal government and public health officials lean strongly towards regulation and have been restricting the marketing of vaping products.

In Britain, e-cigarettes are more celebrated as an aide to help smokers stop their addiction to smoking tobacco, which kills more than 8 million people a year, according to the World Health Organisation.

E-cigarettes first hit the market about a decade ago, and the first versions were clunky, fist-sized devices that users filled with fluid that they usually bought separately.

Now the dominant products are prefilled, pod-based devices such as Juul, which resemble computer flash drives. Other versions look like fancy fountain pens or plastic cigarettes. Some produce a large cloud of vapour, while others allow users to exhale a stream that's nearly invisible.

Where's the danger?

Most people know that smoking is dangerous. Tobacco contains nicotine, one of the most addictive chemical substances known, and delivers other chemicals that cause lung disease, heart disease and more than a dozen different cancers.

But e-cigarette "juice" also contains nicotine, and sometimes a vape delivers much more nicotine than a cigarette. The flavours used in e-cigarette liquids are not well studied, but an outbreak of severe lung disease linked to vaping has put more than 2,600 people into hospitals in the United States and killed around 60.

The U.S. Centers for Disease Control and Prevention has found strong evidence that an oily compound called vitamin E acetate, used in the production of some vaping fluids, is causing the lung damage.

Vitamin E acetate is safe to eat, but there's almost no research showing what it does when inhaled into the lungs. The same goes for most, if not all, the flavourings used in e-cigarettes. This includes THC, the active ingredient in cannabis that is an increasingly popular vape additive.

> 'The damage can be short or long-term.'

At first, doctors, public health experts and others embraced vaping as a safer alternative to smoking. It seemed that if smokers could switch to the seemingly cleaner e-cigarettes as a way to get their nicotine fix, it would save lives.

Public Health England, the government public health agency for England, issued a report in 2015 that said e-cigarettes are 95% safer than traditional cigarettes.

But it can take years for research to catch up to what's happening in the real world.

Now researchers are finding that vaping can cause not only immediate health effects, such as the acute lung injuries seen in the United States, but also longer-term damage.

At the end of 2019, a team at the University of California San Francisco found that people who vape raise their risk of chronic lung diseases such as emphysema, asthma and chronic obstructive pulmonary disease by a third. People who both vaped and smoked more than tripled their risk.

What is more, vaping did not help most smokers quit. Fewer than 1% of smokers switched exclusively to vaping over three years, the researchers found.

Are there really any benefits to vaping?

'One of the biggest problems with e-cigarettes is that many people have switched to e-cigarettes believing it will help them quit tobacco products, which it doesn't,' said Dr. Albert Rizzo, chief medical officer at the American Lung Association. WHO agrees the evidence is murky.

And there's evidence that vaping is even more addictive than smoking. Juuls, for instance, use a formulation of nicotine called nicotine salts that make the product taste smoother and are absorbed more quickly into the body.

Luka Kinard started using e-cigarettes when he was in high school in North Carolina and now speaks frequently in public about his addiction. It took him 40 days in a rehabilitation programme to kick the habit.

'I thought Juuling was safer and even healthier than other tobacco products. But really, I had no idea what I was putting in my body,' he said.

> 'Big Tobacco controls much of the vaping industry.'

It's becoming clear that vaping appeals most strongly to older teens and young adults. The U.S. National Academies commissioned a comprehensive report that found in 2018 that e-cigarette use was encouraging young people who never smoked before to try cigarettes.

While there still may be some debate over whether e-cigarettes can help smokers quit, there's almost universal agreement that non-smokers, especially children, teens and young adults, should not use them at all.

Yet in the United States, where vaping is marketed the most aggressively, there's an epidemic of teen vaping. More than a quarter of U.S. high school students now use vaping products. In response, regulators such as the U.S. Food and Drug Administration are moving to ban the fruit- and candy-flavoured products that are most attractive to young people.

Who profits?

But the big tobacco companies that control much of the vaping industry want to keep and expand their customer base. They are fighting regulation in Washington and looking for markets elsewhere in the world.

Altria, the U.S. company that split from Marlboro maker Philip Morris in 2007, bought a 35% stake in Juul for nearly $13 billion in 2018. Altria CEO and chair Howard Willard has repeatedly said he wants to accelerate Juul's global growth.

THREE QUESTIONS TO CONSIDER:

- How do you know if a new product is safe?
- Tobacco companies are losing customers. How can they stay profitable?
- What makes vaping so appealing?

15 January 2020

The above information is reprinted with kind permission from *News Decoder*.

www.news-decoder.com

What is Spice and why is the drug so dangerous?

THE CONVERSATION

An article from The Conversation.

By Oliver Sutcliffe, Robert Ralphs

Synthetic cannabis, of which Spice is an example, is linked to serious health issues ranging from difficulties breathing to psychotic episodes. But, despite well-known issues, these drugs are still in demand and homeless people, particularly, are at risk of mental health issues from their use. So what exactly are these drugs made of and why do they cause such violent reactions?

Research suggests Spice is not a single drug, but a range of laboratory-made chemicals that mimic the effects of tetrahydrocannabinol (THC), the main psychoactive component of cannabis; that Spice and other forms of synthetic cannabis are capable of producing much more intense and prolonged effects at much lower doses than natural cannabis. This is because, while the THC in natural cannabis only partially reacts with the body, synthetic cannabis reacts far more fully.

To understand the biology behind the intense reaction to Spice we need to look at the parts of the body's central nervous system that react to cannabis – the cannabinoid receptors – and the chemical part of the drug that reacts with the body – the 'agonist'.

While THC is a 'partial agonist'" (it only partially reacts with cannabinoid receptors), synthetic cannabis is often a 'full agonist'. In this way, the more adverse effects observed with synthetic cannabis use stem from its ability to completely saturate and activate all of the body's cannabinoid receptors at a lower dose.

Although the consequences of long-term regular use are not well defined, experts believe that synthetic cannabis has the potential to develop, or cause a relapse of mental illness, especially if there is a family history of mental disorders.

Where does Spice come from?

In 2008, the first synthetic cannabinoid – which reacts with the body in the same way as cannabis – was identified on the recreational drug market. JWH-018 was an aminoalkylindole originally developed by John Huffman of Clemson University in the US and sold under the brand name: Spice. Aminoalkylindoles – the most common sub-family of synthetic cannabinoids – are produced, in kilogram quantities, through quick and simple chemical reactions using legal substances. These substances are produced on a large scale by chemical companies based in China and then shipped, as bulk powders, to Europe by air or sea. Once in Europe, the synthetic cannabinoids are mixed with (or sprayed onto) plant material using solvents such as acetone or methanol to dissolve the powders. The combination is then dried, packaged and sold as either incense or smoking mixtures.

JWH-018 is now a controlled substance in many countries under narcotics legislation. But the prevalence of next-generation synthetic cannabinoids – now known colloquially as Spice or Mamba – continue to be the largest group of new psychoactive substances (NPS) in common usage. As of December 2015, 14 different sub-families of cannabinoid agonists have been identified – indicating that there are potentially hundreds of these types of substances circulating via the internet and often across international borders.

Why is it so dangerous?

Different brands of smoking mixtures can have very different effects, but the strength of a specific brand appears to owe more to the ratio of cannabinoids to chemically inactive plant material in the mixture, rather than the variation in the chemical structure of compounds themselves. In other words, the specific type of chemical in the mixture is less important than how much chemical there is compared to what has been put in to provide bulk.

Due to the high potency of some synthetic cannabinoids, the amount needed for each 'hit' can be as little as a few tens of milligrams (about the size of a match head). The intoxicating effects of more potent brands – such as Clockwork Orange, Pandora's Box and Annihilation – can be quite overpowering. Some people experience difficulty breathing, rapid heart rate, and shakes and sweats, all of which can lead to severe panic attacks. At higher doses, balance and coordination can be severely affected. Users can experience a loss of feeling and numbness in their limbs, nausea, collapse and unconsciousness.

Continued use of synthetic cannabinoids can cause psychotic episodes, which in extreme cases can last for weeks, and may exacerbate existing mental-health illnesses in susceptible users. But most reports of severe mental health, addiction and acts of violence as a result of regular use tend to be among prisoners and homeless people. These groups are much more likely to report high rates of drug dependency, self-define as having addictive personalities and disclose a range of diagnosed mental-health issues including 'dual diagnosis' (drug dependence and at least one mental-health disorder, or at least two personality or psychotic disorders) and existing offences for violence.

Because of the substantial risks of synthetic cannabinoids, many countries have already outlawed their production, possession and distribution. But it is unlikely that the 'war on drugs' will show any sign of relenting, given the rapidly evolving nature of the recreational drugs market and the lack of globalised drug-control legislation. Only by working collectively can scientists, medical professionals and law makers help to stem the flow of these dangerous compounds before they pose a serious threat to health of vulnerable groups in society.

8 August 2018

Drugs penalties

You can get a fine or prison sentence if you:

- take drugs
- carry drugs
- make drugs
- sell, deal or share drugs (also called 'supplying' them)

The penalties depend on the type of drug or substance, the amount you have, and whether you're also dealing or producing it.

Types of drugs

The maximum penalties for drug possession, supply (selling, dealing or sharing) and production depend on what type or 'class' the drug is

Class	Drug	Possession	Supply and production
A	Crack cocaine, cocaine, ecstasy (MDMA), heroin, LSD, magic mushrooms, methadone, methamphetamine (crystal meth)	Up to 7 years in prison, an unlimited fine or both	Up to life in prison, an unlimited fine or both
B	Amphetamines, barbiuturates, cannabis, codeine, ketamine, methylphenidate (Ritalin), synthetic cannabinoids, synthetic cathinones (for example mepehedrone, methoxetamine)	Up to 5 years in prison, an unlimited fine or both	Up to 14 years in prison, an unlimited fine or both
C	Anabolic steroids, benzodiazepines (diazepam), gamma hydroxybutyrate (GHB), gamma butyrolaction (GBL) piperazines (BZP), khat	Up to 2 years in prison, an unlimited fine or both (except anabolic steroids - it's not an offence to possess them for personal use	Up to 14 years in prison, an unlimited fine or both
Temporary class drugs*	Some methylphenidate substances (ethylphenidate, 3,4-dichloromethylohenidate (HDMP -28), isopropylphenidate (IPP or IPPD), 4-methylmethylpohenidate, ethylnaphthidate, propylphenidate) and their simple derivatives	None, but police can take away a suspected temporary class drug	Up to 14 years in prison, an unlimited fine or both

Psychoactive substances penalties

Psychoactive substances include things like nitrous oxide ('laughing gas').

You can get a fine or prison sentence if you:

- carry a psychoactive substance and you intend to supply it
- make a psychoactive substance
- sell, deal or share a psychoactive substance (also called supplying them)

Psychoactive substances	Possession	Supply and production
Things that cause hallucinations, drowsiness or changes in alertness, perception of time and space, mood or empathy with others.	None, unless you're in prison	Up to 7 years in prison, an unlimited fine or both

Food, alcohol, nicotine, caffeine, medicine and the types of drugs listed above do not count as psychoactive substances.

Possessing drugs

You may be charged with possessing an illegal substance if you're caught with drugs, whether they're yours or not.

If you're under 18, the police are allowed to tell your parent, guardian or carer that you've been caught with drugs.

Your penalty will depend on:

- the class and quantity of drug
- where you and the drugs were found
- your personal history (previous crimes, including any previous drug offences)
- other aggravating or mitigating factors

Cannabis

Police can issue a warning or an on-the-spot fine of £90 if you're found with cannabis.

Khat

Police can issue a warning or an on-the-spot fine of £60 on the first 2 times that you're found with khat. If you're found with khat more than twice, you could get a maximum penalty of up to 2 years in prison, an unlimited fine, or both.

Dealing or supplying drugs

The penalty is likely to be more severe if you are found to be supplying drugs (dealing, selling or sharing).

The police will probably charge you if they suspect you of supplying drugs. The amount of drugs found and whether you have a criminal record will affect your penalty.

www.gov.uk

Myths around drink and drug driving debunked including the 'one pint rule'

By Emma Pengelly

Breaking the law when it comes to drink and drug driving is a serious offence that can cost lives.

All too often we hear guilty pleas to drink driving and in the worst case, fatalities caused by driving under the influence.

But how well do you know the law when it comes to drink and drug driving?

There are several misconceptions and little known facts about exceeding the limits, so SurreyLive has enlisted the help of a motoring law expert and a Surrey Roads Policing Unit sergeant to debunk these myths.

To test whether drivers are over the limit, the police can measure how much alcohol you have consumed by taking breath tests, and blood and urine samples.

The limits for each test are as follows:

Per 100ml of breath, 35 micrograms of alcohol is the limit.

Per 100ml of blood, 80 milligrammes of alcohol is the limit.

Per 100ml of urine, 107 milligrammes is the limit.

Let's get to the myths.

1. The limits are the same wherever I drive in the UK

Wrong. In Scotland the limits are a lot lower. The above figures are for England, Wales and Northern Ireland.

But in Scotland, per 100ml of breath 22 micrograms of alcohol is the limit. Per 100ml of blood, 50 milligrammes of alcohol is the limit. Per 100ml of urine, 67 milligrammes is the limit.

If you have been banned by any UK court due to drink driving, you cannot drive anywhere in the UK.

2. I am safe to drive the morning after

This is false.

Surrey Roads Policing Unit sergeant Dan Pascoe said it is "impossible" to put a figure on how many hours it is safe to drive after consuming drink or drugs because "there are so many variables".

He said: "Alcohol and drugs are very different. From experience, an absolute minimum of 12 hours from your last alcoholic drink before driving, and longer if consumption has been high. A minimum of 72 hours after taking drugs. Having a shower doesn't help at all."

David Barton, a motoring lawyer with 38 years of experience, said: "What people often do is underestimate how long it takes the body to get rid of alcohol effects.

"It is not the effect of sleep that gets rid of it, it takes time and it all depends on the individual. For example, men do metabolise it quicker than women.

"The rate at which you metabolise the alcohol depends on factors including your body mass, metabolic rate and your age - the older you are the quicker you will metabolise it."

He added that people "underestimate" and "talk it down" the morning after.

"You may feel better because you have slept, but the body is slow sometimes at metabolising the alcohol," he said.

"I have done a lot of cases where some people have had a doze on the train, thinking getting in an hour or so of sleep will help them, but it makes very little difference."

Mr Barton believes drink driving instances have gone down but "morning after offences have gone up".

"There is a far greater awareness about drink driving. But the morning after, people do not know because they have not really kept a careful track of what they have consumed," he said.

3. Water, coffee or food helps me stay below the limit

This is not true. Mr Barton said although the effects of water, coffee or food will make you feel physically better, physiologically your alcohol levels will not have been significantly affected.

He said: "Food makes you feel better but it does not affect the consumption of alcohol. It is the same with coffee. Caffeine will make you feel more alert but it does not affect alcohol levels."

Mr Pascoe agreed it is a myth. He said: "Having a glass of water will do nothing (or very little) to change your blood alcohol limit."

4. Sucking on a coin will give me a more favourable breathalyser test result

This is a myth, and Mr Pascoe has witnessed first-hand individuals attempting to use this 'trick'.

He said: "Sucking on a 2p coin doesn't work. I've watched someone vigorously suck on a dirty 2p coin for 30 minutes while being booked into custody, only for their evidential reading to be higher than the initial (non evidential) roadside reading."

5. The one pint rule

It is generally recognised if you go over a pint you are taking a risk, but this should not be a blanket rule.

This is due to reasons already stated - each individual's limit varies depending on a variety of factors, including age.

Mr Pascoe said: "Each person is different and for some, having a single pint could result in their arrest."

6. What happens if I am in my car, over the limit, but not driving?

You can still be arrested. It is an offence to be in charge of a vehicle while being over the permitted limit.

Mr Barton said he has had cases where this has happened, for example an individual who was drunk and had fallen asleep in their car.

If you are drunk and found to be in charge of the vehicle, you are committing an offence even if the vehicle is not moving.

7. I can only commit a drug driving offence after consuming illegal drugs

Untrue, it is also illegal to drive in England, Scotland and Wales with legal drugs in your system if it impairs your driving.

It is also an offence to drive if you have more than the specified limits of certain drugs in your blood and you have not been prescribed them.

Mr Barton said: "For prescription drugs you can also be over the legal limit. The legal limits for prescribed drugs are set quite high. But I did have one case which involved an individual who had taken too much insulin, which they were taking because they had diabetes."

The police can pull you over and conduct a saliva roadside test to screen for cannabis or cocaine.

If the police officers believe you are unfit to drive because you have taken drugs, they can arrest you and take you to the station for a blood and urine test.

8. Drugs leave my system as quickly as alcohol

It is a myth to think taking drugs on the weekend means you are safe to drive the next Monday.

Unlike alcohol, drugs take days to leave your system and so it can be a while before you are safely within the driving limit.

Mr Barton said: "With cannabis and cocaine the effects of them stay in the body longer than alcohol. If an individual has a smoke on the weekend, three days later they could still be over the limit. Secondary smoking could also be a problem."

9. I am fine if the roadside drug test returns negative

Wrong. Although the roadside drug test can only screen for cocaine and cannabis, the police can arrest you if they think you are unfit to drive and take you to the station for a blood and urine test.

"As the body metabolises, it turns the drugs into other products and blood tests can detect these," said Mr Barton.

10. Can passengers drink while I drive?

Mr Barton said there is no law prohibiting passengers from drinking when you are driving.

However, if you are distracted while behind the wheel the police can prosecute you for careless driving if they believe you are not in control of the vehicle.

"Passengers can do whatever they like. If there are two or three people drinking then yes you do run that risk of being pulled over," Mr Barton said.

And what about the driver drinking at the wheel, but remaining below the limit?

Mr Pascoe said: "There is no specific offence of consuming alcohol while driving, however it is strongly advised against and the driver could be committing other offences."

11. How do I dispute my drink or drug driving charge?

There is very little room for defence when it comes to these offences.

According to Mr Barton, the breathalysers are "second generation devices" which are "very accurate".

"A defence could be 'I was not actually driving'," he said. "You can challenge breath test results, for example, an individual might say 'it must be wrong because I did not drink enough to produce those results' - but this is difficult to make out."

He added: "There is a legal presumption that the result of the devices are accurate. The other possible line of defence is the police did not follow proper procedure."

12. There are more drink driving offences at Christmas

This is hard to answer robustly. But Mr Barton said he has noticed a "little" spike at Christmas, and in the summer - when people are drinking at barbecues or in their gardens.

13. I had an accident that wasn't my fault but I was over the limit

As a driver you will always be tested in an accident.

"If the other driver causes the accident and police arrive they will breathalyse both drivers. If it was not your fault, but you are over the limit, you will still be arrested," Mr Barton said.

28 February 2020

Will the UK legalise cannabis in the next decade?

It remains to be seen if the present government will legalise cannabis, but this shouldn't be ruled out.

Cannabis was added to the Dangerous Drugs Act of 1920 in 1928, but its usage has risen steadily in spite of this. With Brexit on the horizon, there are many political and legal issues which will again be up for debate, and one which is bound to cause controversy is that of legalising cannabis and other drugs.

The subject has become more mainstream as a result of its increased usage as a medicinal treatment and after the Canadian Prime Minister, Justin Trudeau, legalised cannabis in Canada. He believed that legalising the cannabis trade would help to regulate its use and take money out of the criminal empire, but is the UK likely to follow any time soon?

The law on cannabis today

While over 50 per cent of people in the UK are in favour of legalising the recreational use of cannabis and, according to a YouGov poll, nearly 75 per cent support its use for medicinal purposes – it is still a Class B substance. It was briefly reclassified as a Class C under Tony Blair's Labour government, but then brought back up to Class B under

Gordon Brown. This was due to concerns about cannabis and its potential impact on mental health. Although statistics show that while the number of cannabis users reduced between 2006 and 2014, the demand for mental health services increased by 50 per cent.

Because of the continued concerns about and research into the impact cannabis may have on mental health, it is still illegal to possess, use and distribute cannabis, and you can be charged with cultivation of cannabis. People found guilty can have an unlimited fine imposed on them and/or a potential prison sentence of up to 5 years. Being convicted of supplying cannabis could result in a sentence of up to 14 years.

What are the dangers or benefits of cannabis use?

The mental health concerns around cannabis stem from one of the many chemical compounds found in the marijuana plant: THC. This is the psychoactive substance that is responsible for the 'high' users can experience. There is concern that continued and excessive use of cannabis could lead to mental health issues and addiction. There are different types of marijuana that contain varying levels of THC, with 'skunk' being one of the most potent. However, research by the NHS found that compared to alcohol and tobacco, both of which are legal, cannabis is significantly less addictive and has never been directly attributed as a cause of death in the UK.

In recent years, the cannabidiol or CBD component found in cannabis has been increasingly used for its medicinal properties. While research is in its early stages, CBD has been linked to pain relief, anxiety treatment and treating epilepsy.

What would cannabis legalisation look like?

The IEA stated in a 2018 report that cannabis should be classified and regulated between alcohol and tobacco. The minimum age is likely to be 18 and premises would need to be licensed in order to grow, import and/or sell it.

Currently, cannabis can be prescribed for medicinal use, but in 2018 the government released a statement which said there were 'no plans to legalise or decriminalise the drug'. However, given the unpredictability of the UK's political landscape at the moment, it's difficult to predict what will happen next week let alone next year.

8 January 2020

'Legal highs' may be more dangerous than traditional drugs of abuse

THE CONVERSATION

An article from The Conversation.

By Colin Davidson, Professor of Neuropharmacology, University of Central Lancashire

Novel psychoactive substances (NPS), or 'legal highs', have had various definitions but can simply be thought of as new drugs of abuse. Some may be entirely new, some may be designed to mimic existing drugs, some are based on psychoactive plants and some are medicines.

In the UK, most were legal up until the 2016 Psychoactive Drugs Act, which has effectively banned all drugs which have a psychoactive effect, except alcohol, nicotine, caffeine and drugs used for medicinal purposes. Despite this, they remain widely, albeit illegally, available.

Drug users are a heterogeneous group: many have continued to use traditional drugs of abuse, such as cocaine and heroin, but others have embraced legal highs. It was estimated in 2014 that nearly half of all drug users in the UK have taken an NPS.

The reasons for their popularity include the misconception that because they were once legal they are safe, the ease of obtaining them, and a subset of drug abusers who are "novelty seekers" and want to try something new and exciting.

Prior to 2016, NPS were typically banned as individual drugs or more recently, as groups of chemically related compounds. This led to the synthesis and marketing of an NPS to take the place of the banned substance, while the novelty seekers also drove a market for new drugs.

Unfortunately, we now have close to 700 NPS and this has exacerbated the health risk because, with a new drug, users are unsure how to take it safely and healthcare workers will also know very little about the drug, making effective treatment difficult. A legal high user in A&E might be reliant on medical staff who only have a packet of powder with an unhelpful street name such as 'Ivory Wave' to go on.

We're familiar with the side effects that come from long-term abuse of traditional drugs. Ketamine can lead to bladder problems and incontinence, amphetamines can kill nerve

cells in a process called neurotoxicity, cannabis can increase the risk of developing schizophrenia-like symptoms, MDMA may lead to heart valve problems and numerous drugs lead to addiction.

The mechanisms underlying these problems are largely known and so we can predict the long-term problems of NPS use.

How legal highs affect the body

Synthetic cannabinoids were developed as a legal alternative to cannabis. The main psychoactive compound in cannabis is THC, which activates a cannabinoid receptor protein called CB1.

Spice or K2 has been found to be made up of a variety of synthetic cannabinoids, which are often more than ten times as potent at the CB1 receptor.

The same dose of Spice will have a much bigger effect than the same dose of THC and long-term users of spice may therefore have a greater chance of developing schizophrenia than cannabis users.

Animal studies have long shown that amphetamine compounds can cause neurotoxicity, and may mean long-term amphetamine abusers have persistent dysfunction in their brain dopamine systems.

Dopamine is not only the 'reward' chemical in the brain, but is also critical to movement. Parkinson's patients have part of their brain dopamine system destroyed, leading to problems initiating movement. More recently, studies have found long-term amphetamine users have a greater chance of developing Parkinson's disease, confirming what we'd already seen with animals.

One of the most popular NPS since 2008 has been mephedrone, also known as MCAT or meow meow. Mephedrone is a synthetic drug, similar to the plant-based chemical cathinone. It is a stimulant, like amphetamine, and has a very similar effect in rats and mice and could also leave users with a greater chance of developing Parkinson's.

Examples abound of NPS which might be more dangerous than the drugs they were developed to replace. Desoxypipradrol (Ivory Wave) may be more likely to lead to psychosis than cocaine. Benzofury, an MDMA-like drug, may also cause heart valve problems, Mexxy (methoxetamine), a ketamine-like drug, may also cause bladder problems.

Adding the relative ignorance among users and healthcare professionals about how to take these new drugs safely and how to treat overdoses, it's clear that 'legal highs' are anything but a safe substitute for traditional drugs of abuse.

19 September 2018

War on drugs failing: decriminalise possession says UK committee

The Health Committee has said the UK's war on drugs is failing as drug related deaths are now a public emergency.

By Stephanie Price

In a call for radical change to UK drugs policy the Health Committee of MPs has said the UK war on drugs is failing and has recommended decriminalising drug possession for personal use.

This year the UK saw its highest ever levels of drug related deaths – making the UK the country with the highest number in Europe, three times higher than the average. Deaths in England rose to 2,670 in 2018; an increase of 16% since 2017. The majority of these deaths were opiate related.

The committee also recommends increasing the funding available as a matter of urgency in order to ensure that heroin assisted treatment, naloxone, and needle and syringe programmes are available.

UK war on drugs failing

The report acknowledges the UK's failing war on drugs – noting that the Modern Crime Prevention Strategy states that offenders who regularly use heroin, cocaine and crack cocaine commit an estimated 45% of acquisitive crime and that 'the cartels and dealers leave a worldwide trail of misery, death and corruption.'

Vulnerable and young people are exploited as part of the illegal drugs trade and the UK has seen a 'County Lines' crisis – whereby young people and vulnerable adults are exposed to physical, mental and sexual abuse, and in some instances, will be trafficked to areas a long way from home as part of a network's drug dealing business.

The Mayor of London, Sadiq Khan, recently lifted the lid on the true scale of the impact of County Lines activity with new figures revealing there are more than 4,000 young people involved in lines operating out of London and across the country.

London is the highest exporting area for so-called County Lines – with 15% of all activity originating from the capital and driving gang-related violence and the criminal exploitation of vulnerable young people.

Networks use several methods to groom young people and vulnerable adults, often through the offer of money or drugs, and they are approached in schools, Pupil Referral Units, youth clubs and food outlets, and promised a fake lifestyle that promises benefitting financially from County Lines exploitation.

Decriminalising drug possession

Currently it is illegal to be in possession of any amount of drugs for personal use, and the new recommendations suggest that possession of drugs for personal use should be changed from a criminal to a civil matter. The call is a bid to help reduce the amount of drug related deaths and drug related crime.

The report recommends that the Government should examine the Portuguese system, where decriminalisation was implemented as part of a comprehensive approach to drugs, noting that: 'Decriminalisation of possession for personal use saves money from the criminal justice system and allows for more investment in prevention and treatment.'

The report states: 'The evidence we have heard leads us to conclude that UK drugs policy is failing.

'We recommend a radical change in UK drugs policy from a criminal justice to a health approach. A health focused and harm reduction approach would not only benefit those who are using drugs but reduce harm to and the costs for their wider communities. Responsibility for drugs policy should move from the Home Office to the Department of Health and Social Care.

'We recommend that the Government should consult on the decriminalisation of drug possession for personal use from a criminal offence to a civil matter. The Government should examine the Portuguese system, where decriminalisation was implemented as one part of a comprehensive approach to drugs, including improving treatment services, introducing harm reduction interventions, and better education, prevention and social support.'

Holistic approach to care

Many people who are dependent are living with chronic conditions and have related underlying mental health problems, however, they are not receiving the support they need. As the current guidelines for treating drug dependent individuals are not delivering, the committee wants the Government to look at taking a more holistic approach.

According to the report drug treatment services have faced funding cuts of 27% over the past three years, and notes that dependency on prescription medicines is an emerging and worrying issue which requires greater attention from Government.

The report states: "Decriminalisation of possession for personal use saves money from the criminal justice system that is more effectively invested in prevention and treatment. Decriminalisation will not be effective without investing in holistic harm reduction, support and treatment services for drug addiction. Doing so would save lives and provide better protection for communities."

The report also recommends that Drug Consumption Rooms (DCRs) should be introduced on a pilot basis in areas of high need, accompanied by robust evaluation of their outcomes.

Government priorities

The report has recommended a number of priorities the Government should act on:

- Develop a comprehensive response to drugs, to invest in existing drug treatment services, and extend and develop harm reduction initiatives;
- Fund a comprehensive package of education, prevention and support measures focused on prevention of drug use amongst young people;
- A comprehensive response should also include a focus on improving the life chances of people who are recovering from drug use;
- Reframe drug use as a health rather than a criminal justice issue;
- Decriminalisation must only be introduced as one part of a full, comprehensive approach to drugs; and
- Any reforms should also be supported by rigorous evaluation which gathers longitudinal data on defined outcome measures.

The opioid crisis

Opioids have caused devastation across America where their use has been declared a national health crisis. Over the last year there has been growing concern that the UK is heading in the same direction. The increasing number of people over 40 seeking treatment is raising fears that ageing opiate users with complex needs will come to dominate demand on substance misuse services in future.

In its advice to the Home Secretary earlier this year, the ACMD raised concerns that this group is being failed in their recovery from substance misuse, as services are not catering for their additional needs.

Chair of the ACMD, Dr Owen Bowden-Jones, said: "This ageing cohort is likely to dominate future demand on substance misuse facilities which is why more needs to be done now to help these people access services that meet their needs.

"Government, commissioners and services need to urgently re-assess how to best manage the complex needs of this ageing group.

"The ACMD commissioned the report to investigate the changing age profiles of those seeking treatment for drug use and explain why current services are not meeting their needs."

Another review has linked growing opioid use to poverty, it notes:

- prescribing rates and duration of prescription are higher in some of the most deprived areas of England;
- a similar pattern is also seen for the number of medicines co-prescribed (for example, at least 2 of the drugs);
- for opioids and gabapentinoids, the prescribing rate in the most deprived quintile was 1.6 times the rate in the least deprived quintile; and
- the co-prescribing rate in the most deprived quintile was 1.4 times higher than in the least deprived quintile (30% compared to 21%).

24 October 2019

The above information is reprinted with kind permission from *Health Europa*.

www.healtheuropa.eu

Who is affected by drug addiction and what are the consequences?

With so much stigma attached to drug addiction, most people believe that it is an affliction rather than an illness. Even though addiction is a recognised illness of the brain, it is viewed by most in a bad light. Negative stereotyping has helped to forge opinions and many believe that those affected by addiction are 'bad' or 'weak' individuals. This is not the case. So, who is affected by drug addiction and what are the negative consequences of this illness?

Why do some individuals develop a drug addiction?

Not everyone who uses drugs will go on to suffer with addiction. In fact, there are many people who can use illegal drugs recreationally without ever developing a physical dependence. Then again, there are some who are hooked after just one use. So why does this happen?

There is no single cause of addiction, and scientists have so far been unable to pinpoint any reason why some people are affected by addiction while others are not. What they do know, however, is that there are certain factors that increase the likelihood of an individual being affected.

Having said that, even having every single risk factor does not make a person a certainty for addiction. There are some people who will never be affected by addiction despite having every factor that is deemed to increase their likelihood of becoming an addict. There are others with no risk factors but who will end up being destroyed by addiction. The reality is that anyone who uses mood-altering substances is at risk of addiction. They are all capable of allowing their use of these substances to spiral out of control to the point where addiction cripples them.

The risk factors of addiction

Scientists have discovered that there are certain risk factors that make a person more likely to develop addiction. Some of these factors are:

- **Early Exposure** – The younger a person is when he or she tries drugs, the more likely this individual is to be affected by addiction when older. Most addicts began using drugs before they were eighteen.
- **Family History** – Having a family history of addiction increases the risk of a person being affected. You might think that children of addicts would be the ones who would avoid drugs themselves when older having seen the damage that can be done, but the reality is that having an addicted parent increases the likelihood of being affected in later life.

- **Mental Health Problems** – Mental health problems and addiction tend to go hand-in-hand. Those who suffer with illnesses such as anxiety disorder or chronic depression will often self-medicate with mood-altering substances such as illegal drugs. It must also be mentioned that many individuals who abuse these substances will then go on to suffer mental health problems including psychosis, schizophrenia, and dementia.
- **Trauma** – Traumatic experiences contribute to the development of addiction in many people. Trauma can leave them feeling vulnerable and anxious, leaving many to self-medicate with substances such as drugs and alcohol. Traumatic experiences include physical, sexual and emotional abuse, being bullied, the loss of a loved one, childhood neglect, having a mentally ill or incarcerated relative, or witnessing combat.

Who does addiction affect?

Absolutely anyone can be affected by addiction. It is easy to assume that drug addicts are from deprived neighbourhoods with very little prospect in life, but this is not always the case. In fact, many drug addicts are just like everyone else; they have loving families, nice homes, good jobs, and financial stability. To the outside world, they might even appear to have it all.

Contrary to popular belief, addiction affects individuals of all ages, races, religions, and backgrounds. It does not discriminate based on where a person lives or how much money he or she has. That does not stop others from forming an opinion of what an addict looks or acts like. Many people believe that all drug addicts:

- are known to the police and have a history of criminal activity
- steal money from their family and friends
- are unable to hold down a job
- spend most of their time injecting drugs down dark alleyways
- do not wash or take care of grooming
- have no prospects in life
- have left school early
- are homeless or are living in squats with other drug addicts.

The danger of stereotyping addicts is that many of these affected individuals will continue with their addictive behaviour as they do not see themselves as addicts. Some will never reach out for help for their addiction due to worrying what others will think of them if it is discovered that he or she has an addiction.

Stereotyping of addiction can lead to discrimination and hatred and can severely impact an individual's chance for recovery. Many people believe that addicts are to blame for their situation and so they have no compassion for the addicted person's plight. They fail to realise that addiction is an illness, just as diabetes or the flu are illnesses. Addiction is not a choice; if it were, why would anyone choose it? It destroys lives and those affected have no control over their ability to quit. Even when they want to stop taking drugs, they are compelled to keep using because of the changes to the structure of their brain.

The impact of addiction

Drug addiction has a massive negative impact on the life of the affected individual. It leads to poor health and is linked to many physical and mental health problems. Those who take illegal drugs always have the worry of overdose hanging over them.

Many street drugs are mixed with other substances by dealers who want to stretch their profits. This means that these substances range in purity and constituents. Those who are used to a drug of a certain purity, for example, could overdose on a batch of drugs that are stronger than those they are used to.

The family members of drug addicts will also have to live with the constant fear of someone knocking on their door to tell them their addicted loved one is dead. This can lead to massive amounts of stress and can result in various health problems. It is difficult to watch a loved one destroy their life knowing that there is absolutely nothing that can be done to help.

Family members often become obsessed with trying to help the affected individual, and their life will begin to revolve around the addicted family member. They are often described as being co-dependent; they also have an addiction, but it is to the addict and not a substance.

Other family members will become defensive and angry with the addict or may blame themselves for their loved one's actions. Many constantly ask themselves if there was anything that could have been done differently to prevent the addiction from developing.

Children of addicts are particularly affected, with many going on to suffer with lasting emotional problems in later life. Young children may not understand what is happening with their parent and will be confused by the parent's erratic behaviour. They may feel lonely, isolated, and neglected, and some will become withdrawn or even manipulative in their efforts to get what they need to survive. These traits can extend into adulthood and can affect their ability to form healthy relationships with their peers.

The effect of drug addiction on the individual and his or her family is massive, but the damage does not stop there. Addiction often negatively affects close friends and colleagues as well; the wider community is affected too. Drug addiction is a major contributing factor in many violent crimes, with many prisoners in the UK affected by addiction. It is true that in over half of all violent crimes the victim believed that the perpetrator was under the influence of drugs or alcohol.

Drug addiction drains public services such as the National Health Service and police resources. Drug-related illnesses and injuries are placing a massive strain on the NHS, and drug-related crimes are taking up valuable police resources. As well as the time that is devoted to substance-related issues, there is also a huge cost to the economy. Substance abuse and addiction costs the UK economy billions of pounds every single year.

Overcoming a drug addiction

The good news is that help is available for those who want to put their days of substance abuse to bed once and for all. Provided an individual is motivated to succeed and willing to make necessary changes to his or her life, he or she can look forward to a new and healthy way of living.

It is true that services such as drug detox and rehab are vital, but they are severely underfunded. Those who manage to overcome their addictions often go on to become valuable members of society. If they stay sober, they can live productive lives with their families and some even go on to become pillars of their communities.

Failure to get help for addiction can mean that some addicts will succumb to their illness. They will never reach their potential and will spiral further into the depths of addiction.

With a drug detox, the addict will be separated from the substance to which he or she is addicted. During this process, it is likely that various withdrawal symptoms will occur. For most people, these symptoms will be mild to moderate in intensity, but the potential for severe symptoms will always be present. These symptoms can include seizures and convulsions, so for the comfort and safety of the addict, it is best to detox in a supervised facility.

Detox programmes typically last between seven and ten days, during which time the withdrawal symptoms will reach a peak before subsiding. After the patient has completed the detox, he or she will be ready to get started on tackling the psychological side of the illness; this takes place with rehabilitation.

Rehab programmes for drug addiction are either inpatient or outpatient based. Most outpatient programmes are provided by charities, local support groups, and the NHS, although there are a number of private counsellors in any given area who also offer outpatient programmes to those in need of help.

Inpatient programmes tend to be the remit of the private clinic and are considered by many as the best way to get started on the road to recovery. This is because these facilities offer an intensive and time-consuming approach to getting well. The programmes typically last between six and eight weeks during which time patients will leave their everyday lives and move into the clinic for the duration of their treatment. They will live with other recovering addicts in a distraction-free environment where they have no access to temptations or triggers and little choice but to concentrate on recovery.

Bring ex-addicts on board to tackle drug deaths crisis, say experts

Speakers make plea ahead of separate summits by Scottish and UK governments in Glasgow.

By Libby Brooks

Crisis levels of drug-related deaths in Scotland, and across the UK, can only be tackled if people with experience of addiction and recovery have a seat at the table, according to speakers ahead of two major conferences in Glasgow this week.

In a sign of escalating tensions between the Scottish and UK governments, summits on the spiralling death toll from drugs, organised separately by each administration, will take place at the same city centre venue on Wednesday and Thursday.

Jardine Simpson of the Scottish Recovery Consortium said: "There's been a lot of talk about the timing of the conferences, but the real story here is still drug deaths and the desperate need to reinvent the narrative around addiction and recovery. Addiction is an isolating experience in itself, but when society rejects you it is doubly stigmatising."

Simpson will speak at Wednesday's summit, organised by the Scottish government in partnership with Glasgow's city council, which has led calls for a pilot drug consumption room, so far denied by Westminster. It has also set up the first heroin-assisted treatment centre in Scotland, as drug deaths and HIV infection rates in Glasgow soar.

Reflecting the concerns of many in the recovery movement, Simpson said: "Of course people should be offered medically assisted treatment [usually methadone], but most people who come forward for help ultimately want to be substance-free. They need psycho-social support too, but our services don't currently deliver both."

"You Keep Talking, We Keep Dying" is the stark slogan of the campaign set up by Faces and Voices of Recovery UK (Favor UK) as a response to the 27% increase in drug-related deaths in Scotland over the last recorded year – alongside a 16% increase in deaths from drug poisoning in England and Wales, the highest annual leap since records began.

In the past 12 months, the Scottish affairs select committee has concluded its inquiry into problem drug use, the Scottish government drug deaths taskforce has been convened, and Dame Carol Black has concluded her year-long review into drug use and supply across the UK, the findings of which will be delivered at Thursday's summit.

But there is a growing anger among charities and specialists at what they see as political inertia beyond this high-level talk on both sides of the border, as well as frustration that improvements that could be made right now are overshadowed by wrangling about Westminster's intransigence in refusing to devolve drug laws to Scotland.

Annemarie Ward of Favor UK, a delegate to the Scottish government summit, argues that the current system is unbalanced with too much focus on managing symptoms, be that methadone, heroin-assisted treatment or safe injecting facilities: "What we call treatment in the UK is actually harm reduction intervention. We need the same size of investment to pay for detox, rehab and trauma therapy."

Other practitioners argue that improving access to medical treatment is essential for those who are not ready or capable of engaging with more intensive therapies. A further rise in death rates is anticipated this year, the result of a "perfect storm" of unpredictably strong prescription drugs flooding the market, poly-drug use and decades-long addicts in already fragile health.

Martin Powell of the drug policy foundation Transform, another delegate at the Scottish summit, noted with optimism that the UK event would hear a presentation from Portugal's ministry of health about that country's world-leading decriminalisation experience.

"We have a lot to learn from Portugal [in terms of prosecutions], but the UK government should allow safer drug consumption room pilots, to engage the hard to reach people who inject alone and on the street.

"We need funding for a lot more heroin prescribing clinics like those in Glasgow and Middlesbrough, which save lives, reduce HIV infections and crime to fund use, while taking money from the heroin trade away from organised crime. We also need places people can get their drugs tested so they know what they are taking and don't overdose accidentally: the UK government licensed a pilot of this in Weston-super-Mare last year."

The prominence of international perspectives, along with expectations that Black's review of current policy will be fairly critical, has led some observers to speculate that the UK government may be ready to signal a shift. The UK crime minister, Kit Malthouse, who will be chairing Thursday's event, has supported diversion schemes such as those piloted in the Thames Valley and Durham that aim to break the cycle of addiction and crime by directing those caught with small amounts of drugs for personal use towards treatment and education.

Another international expert speaking at the UK government event is Keith Humphreys, a Stanford University professor who advised Barack Obama on drugs policy. He told *The Guardian* that he planned to challenge the UK government to give Scotland's recovery community "a seat at the table".

"While medication and treatment are essential services, most people seeking help desire more than just biological stabilisation and reduced drug use/harm – they want a full life, connection to other people and community, and a productive role in the world: in other words they want recovery."

25 February 2020

www.theguardian.com

'At 9 I started becoming addicted to drugs. 42 years later I've turned my life around'

'For years, my life just spiralled out of control. Now I'm on the other side, I can see it was never together anyways.'

By Jasmine Andersson

John has been homeless, imprisoned and lost contact with his family because of his life-defining drug addiction. Now, he is turning his life around and spending the next nine months training to become an electrician.

I'm a born and bred East Londoner, and lived in Hackney Downs until I left home at 15. I am an only child, and I was raised by my mum and stepfather - if I can use that word. It felt more like I was more dragged up than brought up.

My stepfather was very violent. He was an alcoholic. From when I was about three years old, he attacked me and my mother, until I left home at 15. For a young child, it was a very fearful place. Every day, I wasn't allowed to talk unless I was spoken to, and if I broke the rules, I was stamped on and thrown against the walls. When I was fed, I was made to eat the food off the floor with the dogs.

My mum was getting her face smashed in on a daily basis. I grew up feeling very scared, and it was hard knowing that I couldn't protect my mum. I tried a number of times, but I was only a child, and he was around 20 stone, so it didn't really work.

'Soon enough, I became a feral kid'

It was a never a happy home. I grew up with no self worth, self esteem, because I was put down all the time. I think because I wasn't my stepdad's son, he couldn't deal with me. I remember being called a bastard child, and not knowing what that word meant. I later found out that my mum had been raped and fell pregnant with me, and that's what he was getting at.

My experience made me feel different from everybody else. It felt like all of my other friends had a nice home, and they were nurtured. Mine was totally the opposite. To people on the outside, like the neighbours, they didn't realise anything was wrong.

I told my friends exactly what was going on, but I didn't know an adult I could trust to tell. My auntie saw the way my stepfather acted towards her sister, but she was scared of him as well.

Soon enough, I became a feral kid. I stayed out of the house as much as possible, going out as early as I could and stay out as late as possible. My friends became my family.

'I was four foot tall, going out to buy drugs from the main road'

Like a lot of kids at that age, you do what your friends do. Because my friends did drugs, I ended up getting involved with drugs. I have memories when of me being about nine years old, just four foot tall, and going out to buy drugs from a main road nearby. After that, things got blurry. But because we all took drugs, I felt part of something. It was something I felt part of for the first time in my life.

I left home at the age of 15. At this point, I'd grown, and I wasn't scared of my stepfather any more. I had fights, and he couldn't take it. One time, it got so heated my mum took a knife to her wrists, and cut them. She collapsed in a pool of blood. After my stepdad watched her fall to the ground, he stepped over her body and left me with her.

When she came back, about a week later, we argued for the week. She said I'd ruined her life, I was the reason he left, and she kicked out the house. I started thinking was it me, am I such a waste of life, that's what my mum actually thinks. From there, one of my mate's mums passed away. I went to live with him in that room in the 4 bed. To survive, I started selling cannabis just to make money.

From the age of nine, I drank, smoked cannabis, and my addiction just progressed. By my early teens I was taking cocaine, pills, and then by 16, heroin. By the age of 17, I was physically addicted. For years, my life just spiralled out of control. Now I'm on the other side, I can see it was never together anyways.

Then my life went downhill very rapidly after heroin. I started committing horrendous crimes to fund it. Inevitably, I ended up in prison, and then my life just entered this damaging cycle. I'd go to prison, come out, and use, and then I'd get arrested and go back to jail. A lot of the time, I'd have nowhere to go and end up homeless, then you're back in that cycle again. The only thing you know, that you care about, is where your next fix is. I had nowhere to live, so I had to go back to where I know, with my friends who are users, and then you're on that roundabout again.

'I had plenty of rock bottoms over the years'

I had plenty of rock bottoms over the years. When I was sent down for armed robbery in 2013, I was ordered to serve six years and eight months in prison. But still, I couldn't stop using. Drugs were all around me inside and outside. It was only at that point I realised how big my problem had got: I got sent to prison for using drugs, and I'm still using them.

I took part in a substance abuse dependency treatment programme for six months, and that made me understand I am dealing with a disease. It's an obsession of the mind. I didn't choose to have it, who would?

I used to pray every night for god to take me in my sleep. I would wake up in the morning, and ask why god hadn't listened, because I just knew I'd use again.

'I love my life today'

My life changed when I got clean on 27 November 2016. I know the date off by heart. I was getting released the following Friday, and I wasn't looking forward to it at all. I knew what I was going back out to, and I could see the cycle all over again. I saw it repeating and repeating, and I thought "this time, you might not end up back in prison, you'll just end up dead."

I thought I need to do this for me, I deserve better. Something clicked and I thought, it's only me who's going to better my life. I arranged to go into a treatment centre to stop the addiction. When I looked into treatment centres outside, I found out I needed to be clean to go through the programme. With that motivation, I did all the withdrawals myself, which is harder than it seems when temptation is all around you, and everyone in prison is using drugs.

I live in supported housing now, and I'm very grateful to have a roof over my head. It was the housing agency that referred me to Beam, who laid out my career options. I used to work as a roofer and run my own business. But maintaining a business with an active addition didn't work out well for me. I'm a roofer who learned it on the side. I didn't have a clue what practical work I could qualify for at 51, but a support assistant came and sat down with me, and he's gone through different jobs and so forth, he really suggested becoming an electrician. It really kind of piqued my interest. It's a great place, and I'm really excited now, to finally have a plan and have some focus on where my life is going to go. I know in 3 years' time, I will be running my own business and hiring electricians. I will be qualified up to the eyeballs.

Since I've been in recovery, I've rebuilt relationships with my four children. When you're an addict, you neglect the ones you love. Even with my mum, we're in communication, and working on our relationship. I've got two grand-kids now, aged four and seven. Being a granddad is the best feeling in the world. It's nice because they've never seen me use. They've just seen their granddad and that's lovely.

I love my life today. I managed to get myself to the place where I could have always been, and the person I wanted to be honest hardworking, trustworthy human being, not a lowlife junkie. That's how I used to look at myself. I never had no empathy for myself. But I have today. I think about me, as a little boy. That little boy couldn't defend himself. He had no one to help him, to nurture him. I don't let that define me any more. All that childhood defined me, then the drugs defined me. I've grown so much in the past three odd years. I can't change the past, no matter what. But I can certainly change my future.

24 January 2020

Residential addiction services in England cut by third amid drug overdose and funding crisis, figures show

'Considering that there is a crisis of drug related deaths in this country, these figures could not be more shocking.'

By Alex Matthews-King

The number of live-in drug and alcohol rehabilitation services in England has fallen by one-third in six years, according to a new analysis which reveals the damaging toll of austerity cuts as drug deaths soar.

There were 195 residential rehabilitation and detox services registered with the Care Quality Commission (CQC) in England in 2013, but by 2019 this had fallen to just 132 active centres.

Rehabilitation centres are typically run by charities or private companies, but many rely on councils to fund placements for people with addiction issues.

Experts have warned that as budgets fall councils are sending more people to cheaper community-based rehabilitation, including day centres and groups.

While community services can provide support for some, treatment providers and people who have used residential rehabilitation say it is still an integral part of addiction, and can be 'lifesaving'.

'I don't think looking at my journey into recovery that it would have ever started if I had been asked to do my detox and rehabilitation in the community,' Peter Krykant, 42, told *The Independent*.

At the turn of the millennium Mr Krykant had been homeless for three years after moving to Birmingham from Scotland. He was receiving prescription methadone, and benzodiazepines, in addition to 'vast amounts of heroin and crack cocaine', but a grant through the city's rough sleepers team funded a place at the Princess Diana Drug and Alcohol Treatment Centre – which has since closed.

'There's no way that would happen now,' Mr Krykant said. 'People need to tick so many boxes and if you're entrenched in street drug use, crime, homelessness, there's no way that people who are the hardest to reach are getting access to residential treatment.

'That's my bugbear.'

He said residential rehabilitation, which is an opportunity for counselling alongside addiction treatments, particularly benefits people who may have had traumatic experiences that led to their drug use, or resulted from it.

'We are so superficial in the way we deal with people who are addicted to drugs and alcohol that we don't give them opportunities to really change when we don't give them that space and time.

'A lot of money was spent on me to go through that but I've now been paying into the system for many years.'

The fall comes as councils in England struggle to maintain services in the face of swingeing government cuts.

Drug deaths in England and Wales have set new records in each of the last four years. This is driven by rising abuse of potent opioid painkillers like fentanyl and an ageing generation of lifelong heroin users.

Despite this, spending on both residential rehab and detox services, as well as community rehabilitation schemes, has fallen by as much as £135m according to an analysis of council spending by private rehabilitation provider UK Addiction Treatment Centres.

The result is councils are less willing to place people in residential centres, and eventually they may be forced to close. UKAT's analysis shows that residential rehabilitation services have fallen from 42 to 18 in London, while in the northeast only one of six centres open in 2013 is still active.

Broadreach House in Plymouth ceased trading in July after nearly 40 years providing rehabilitation to patients across the UK. 'The irony of this predicament is that we are currently at full capacity, with the demand for our services in recent months being greater than ever,' the charity said in a post on Facebook.

Mike Pattinson, executive director of Change Grow Live, one of the largest drug treatment providers in England, told The Independent residential centres continued to play an "integral role" in treatment.

'We regret the continual and almost relentless closure of such services – with Broadreach House and City Roads in London being two of the latest casualties.

'Whilst it is true that residential treatment is more expensive than community-based options, in some circumstances it remains entirely appropriate and can be lifesaving.'

He said the impact of cuts and the decision to shift responsibility for drug treatment and other public health responsibilities to local authorities had been 'felt most acutely' in residential rehab.

Once closed the expertise linked with these services can be gone for good.

'Considering that there is a crisis of drug-related deaths in this country, these figures could not be more shocking,' said Niamh Eastwood of charity Release, which advocates for a public health, rather than criminal justice, approach to drug policy.

But she warned community services had been drastically cut as well, to the extent that some were struggling to provide substitute prescribing of methadone, which can cut heroin overdose deaths.

Cllr Ian Hudspeth, chairman of the Local Government Association's community wellbeing board, said: 'In the past year, local authorities have spent more than £700m on tackling substance misuse.

'However, cuts to councils' public health grant by central government have consequences. We have long argued that reductions to councils' public health funding, which is used to pay for drug and alcohol prevention and treatment services, is a false economy which will only compound acute pressures for criminal justice and NHS services further down the line.

'Leaving councils to pick up the bill for treating new and increasing numbers of users while having fewer resources cannot be an option.'

A Department of Health and Social Care spokesperson said: 'Drug use in this country is lower now than it was a decade ago, with more adults leaving treatment successfully – while alcohol consumption has fallen overall.

'As part of our long term plan for the NHS, alcohol care teams will be rolled out in hospitals with the highest number of alcohol-related admissions and we are also giving £3.5bn to councils this year to fund public health services, including those for addiction.'

13 July 2019

'Dayhab' clinics to offer new way to treat alcohol and drug addictions

By Laura Donelly

Experts say a new network of 'dayhab' centres will offer functioning alcoholics and drug addicts the chance to treat their problems by day, while living at home.

The new chain of private centres, run by a former government advisor who helped Russell Brand come off heroin, says the method will offer therapy at a fraction of the cost of traditional residential programmes.

The first unit, which will open in West London next month, follows warnings that those in their 50s are now most likely to be drinking at harmful levels, as millennials turn their back on such habits.

The chain - called Help Me Stop - is adapted from a US model, which claims three in four participants remain abstinent, nine months after completing the programme.

The chain is aimed at those in senior white-collar professional roles, who are functioning in the workplace, but have a problem with drink or drugs.

It comes after middle-class drug use was at the centre of the Tory leadership campaign, with Michael Gove under particular pressure about his cocaine use.

A five-week, 160-hour programme at Help Me Stop will cost £2,500, compared to typical residential costs of around £25,000.

The programme is adapted from an intensive outpatient treatment model successfully pioneered in the US. Studies from the Twin Town dayhab centre, which has five units in Los Angeles, report continuous abstinence for 76 per cent of clients nine months after completion of treatment – a figure which is comparable to residential outcomes.

Chip Somers, Help Me Stop's clinical director, a former drug addict, who was a member of the government's rehabilitation expert panel between 2007-11, said the programme was 'the first of its kind' in the UK.

He said: 'Not everyone can afford to put their lives on hold for weeks at a time to go to rehab. The beauty of dayhab is that it's designed to fit around daily life: people can stay at home, look after their children, or continue to work or study while receiving treatment. This is rehab in the real world - accessible to all.'

More sites will open across London and the South East of England over the next two years.

Mr Somers said currently those with alcohol or drug problems had few options.

'Local authority services are virtually non-existent, while vastly expensive residential rehab facilities are out of reach for most. It's shocking that less than three per cent of people seeking help for alcohol or drug issues currently receive the treatment they need.'

It comes as figures show a near doubling in the number of over 75s admitted to hospital after taking drugs in the last decade, with experts saying the rise is a legacy of the 'Swinging Sixties'.

The NHS statistics show there were 1,581 hospital admissions by over-75-year-olds related to drug misuse in 2017/8.

Professor Julia Sinclair, chairman of the Royal College of Psychiatrists' addiction faculty, called for the health service to fund more day treatment services.

She said: 'The evidence is that day treatment services can work and that people with drug or alcohol addiction can be treated successfully while staying at home.

'This model of care is recommended by the National Institute for Health and Care Excellence and used to be available in the UK prior to swingeing cuts in recent years to addiction services' budgets.'

'A stay-at-home service which costs a tenth as much as a residential service will be more affordable to some, but there is still the risk of creating a two-tier level of service for people with drug and alcohol addiction.'

Last year 260,153 people received some kind of NHS treatment for drug and alcohol problems, but fewer than 6,000 were placed in residential rehabilitation programmes.

She said: 'The real solution to soaring rates of drug and alcohol addiction – including a 16 per cent rise in alcohol-related deaths since 2007 – is to restore community and inpatient addiction services to the state they were in a decade or more ago. This would involve significant investment.'

22 June 2019

Key Facts

- A person may be either physically addicted, psychologically addicted, or both, depending on which specific substance they consume. (page 1)
- Drug abuse is not the same as drug addiction: it is possible to abuse drugs without being addicted to them. (page 1)
- Some people are genetically more predisposed than others to developing addictions. (page 2)
- In England and Wales during 2018-2019, deaths related to poisoning by drug misuse were 46% higher than they were ten years ago. (page 6)
- 20.3% of young adults aged 16 to 24 have taken an illicit drug in the last year). (page 6)
- In the last year, hospital admissions for poisoning by drug misuse were highest among people aged 25 to 34. (page 7)
- The number of drug-related deaths in Scotland increased by 27% in 2018 to 1,187 - the largest number ever recorded and more than double the number recorded a decade ago. (page 10)
- Nearly 12 million people – about one in four adults – in England are taking medicines for pain, depression or insomnia. (page 13)
- 7.3 million people in England – 17% of the adult population – are on antidepressants. (page 13)
- In 2015 Section 5A of the Road Traffic Act was introduced. This set an upper limit for the level of specific controlled drugs in a driver's blood. (page 15)
- An upper legal limit of 80 milligrammes of alcohol per 100ml (also referred to as 0.08%) of blood was adopted across Europe over 50 years ago. Unlike the rest of Europe and Scotland, the rest of the UK has not changed this legal level. In Scotland, for example it is now 0.05%. (page 15)
- In 2013, the National Transportation Safety Board in the US reduced the legal limit for blood alcohol from 0.08% to 0.05%. This resulted in an 11% decline in fatal alcohol-related crashes. (page 15)
- The number of adults who vape around the world is expected to reach almost 55m by 2021, according to market research group Euromonitor. (page 16)
- Smoking causes nearly 80,000 deaths a year in the UK. (page 16)
- In the UK, 15 per cent of 11-18 year-olds tried vaping in 2019 compared to 16 per cent in the previous year, according to a study conducted by anti-smoking charity Action on Smoking Health. But there was an increase in the number of current vapers in that age group from 5 per cent in 2019 compared to 3 per cent in 2018. (page 18)
- Public Health England, the government public health agency for England, issued a report in 2015 that said e-cigarettes are 95% safer than traditional cigarettes. (page 19)
- At the end of 2019, a team at the University of California San Francisco found that people who vape raise their risk of chronic lung diseases such as emphysema, asthma and chronic obstructive pulmonary disease by a third. (page 19)
- Spice is not a single drug, but a range of laboratory-made chemicals that mimic the effects of tetrahydrocannabinol (THC), the main psychoactive component of cannabis. (page 20)
- You may be charged with possessing an illegal substance if you're caught with drugs, whether they're yours or not. (page 23)
- If you're under 18, the police are allowed to tell your parent, guardian or carer that you've been caught with drugs. (page 23)
- Currently, cannabis can be prescribed for medicinal use, but in 2018 the government released a statement which said there were 'no plans to legalise or decriminalise the drug'. (page 27)
- According to the Health Committee report drug treatment services have faced funding cuts of 27% over the past three years. (page 30)
- There were 195 residential rehabilitation and detox services registered with the Care Quality Commission (CQC) in England in 2013, but by 2019 this had fallen to just 132 active centres. (page 37)
- In 2018, 260,153 people received some kind of NHS treatment for drug and alcohol problems, but fewer than 6,000 were placed in residential rehabilitation programmes. (page 39)

Glossary

Addiction
A dependence on a substance which makes it very difficult to stop taking it. Addiction can be either physical, meaning the user's body has become dependent on the substance and will suffer negative symptoms if the substance is withdrawn, or psychological, meaning a user has no physical need to take a substance, but will experience strong cravings if it is withdrawn.

Amphetamines
Synthetic drugs which can be swallowed, inhaled or injected. Their effects can include increased mental alertness, energy, and confidence. Most amphetamines are Class B substances, but crystal meth and prepared-for-injection speed are Class A. Taking amphetamines can cause anxiety or paranoia and risks include overdose and psychological dependence. They can also put strain on a user's heart, leading to cardiac problems.

Depressant
A substance that slows down the nervous system, making the user feel calmer and more relaxed. These drugs are also known as 'downers' and include alcohol, heroin and tranquilisers.

Detox
Ridding the body of toxins, i.e. drugs.

Drug
A chemical that alters the way the mind and body works. Legal drugs include alcohol, tobacco, caffeine and prescription medicines taken for medical reasons. Illegal drugs taken for recreation include cannabis, cocaine, ecstasy and speed. These illegal substances are divided into three classes – A, B and C – according to the danger they pose to the user and to society (with A being the most harmful and C the least).

Drug driving law
In the UK it is illegal to drive if you are unfit to do so because you are taking legal or illegal drugs, or if you have certain levels of illegal drugs in your blood.

Hallucinogen
A drug which produces visions and sensations detached from reality (a 'trip'). Common hallucinogens include LSD, ketamine and magic mushrooms.

Legal high
Also known as psychoactive substances, legal highs function as stimulants and have mood altering properties.

Misuse of Drugs Act 1971
Legislation prohibiting the use of dangerous recreational substances, making it an offence to possess banned drugs for personal use or with the intent to supply. It also divides drugs into three classes according to the degree of harm they pose to the individual and to society – A, B or C – each with different associated penalties.

Needle exchange
A service that allows drug users to obtain safe, clean hypodermic needles.

Opiate
A drug that is derived from opium, e.g. heroin.

Overdose
This occurs when an individual takes such a large dose of a drug that their body cannot cope with the effects. An overdose can cause organ failure, coma and death.

Psychoactive Substances Act
The Psychoactive Substances Act makes it a criminal offence to produce or supply any psychoactive substance. The Act is designed to stop people from trading in 'legal highs'. Possessing a psychoactive substance will not be an offence.

Rehab
A course of treatment for drug or alcohol dependence, typically at a residential facility.

Stimulant
A volatile substance which gives off fumes. Vapours from products including paint, glue and aerosols can be inhaled and cause intoxication. Volatile substance abuse is highly dangerous and quite often fatal.

Withdrawal
Physical or psychological symptoms experienced following the abrupt discontinuation of a drug to which the user has formed an addiction.

Activities

Brainstorming

- In small groups, discuss what you know about drug use and abuse:
  - Define what a drug is.
  - Why do some people abuse drugs?
  - What is the difference between someone who uses drugs and someone who has an addiction to drugs?
  - What are the negative effects that drug misuse can have on your physical and mental health?
  - Write a list of the risks and consequences of misusing legal and illegal drugs.
  - Write a list of legal and illegal drugs that you are aware of.

Research

- Do some research online looking for articles and information about over-the-counter or prescription drug misuse. What substances seem to be the most commonly abused?
- Research the drugs laws in a different country and write 500 words exploring whether their policy is more or less effective than the policy in the UK.
- Read the article 'Scotland has worst drugs problem in Europe as death rate soars' on page 11. Which drug in particular has contributed the most to the mortality rate? Who makes up the highest proportion of the mortality figures - males or females?
- With a partner, research the different types of treatment programmes for drug addiction that are available in the UK. What do they involve?

Design

- Choose one of the drugs mentioned in the article Drugs and the brain on page 4. Create a poster that illustrates the risks associated with taking your chosen drug.
- Working in small groups of three or four, design a campaign that warns young people about the dangers of risky behaviour such as drug taking. Design your campaign to work across print, broadcast and social media platforms.
- Design a poster aimed at helping people to recognise the signs and symptoms of drug abuse or addiction in a friend or family member. Where do you think would be the best places to display it and why?

Oral

- Imagine you are concerned about your friend's use of cannabis. Write an email to your friend explaining why you are concerned and giving advice about where they could turn for help.
- Refer to the articles on pages 16 and 18 about vaping. In small groups discuss the positive and negative effects of this alternative to cigarette smoking.
- Create a storyboard for a TV ad campaign highlighting the legal consequences of drug use. The campaign should be aimed at teenagers and explain the penalties for using Class A, B and C drugs. Most importantly, it should demonstrate the long-term impact that a criminal record could have on their lives.
- Divide the class into 'Support' and 'Opposition' and hold a debate on the following statement: All drugs should be decriminalised.
- Read the article 'Myths around drink and drug driving...' on page 24 and as a class discuss any other myths relating to alcohol and drug use you have heard about.
- Imagine you are at a party and someone is encouraging you to try a legal or illegal drug. You really don't want to but feel pressurised. In pairs, role-play this scenario and come up with three ways to say 'No' with confidence.

Reading/writing

- Watch the film *Trainspotting*. Is its portrayal of heroin addicts in 90s Edinburgh still relevant to the UK today? Think about the effect that drug abuse has on the characters' relationships, health and lifestyle. Write a review of the film.
- Write a short description about the affect each of the following categories of drugs has on an individual:
  - Depressants
  - Stimulants
  - Hallucinogens
  - Opiates.
- Imagine that you are one of a team of people organising a summer festival. Write a report for your colleagues about the dangers of illegal highs and why you are concerned about their use at the festival. You should include suggestions for steps that could be taken to limit their use.

Index

Acknowledgements

The publisher is grateful for permission to reproduce the material in this book. While every care has been taken to trace and acknowledge copyright, the publisher tenders its apology for any accidental infringement or where copyright has proved untraceable. The publisher would be pleased to come to a suitable arrangement in any such case with the rightful owner.

The material reproduced in *ISSUES* books is provided as an educational resource only. The views, opinions and information contained within reprinted material in *ISSUES* books do not necessarily represent those of Independence Educational Publishers and its employees.

Images

Cover image courtesy of iStock. All other images courtesy of Pixabay, Rawpixel and Unsplash.

Icons

Icons on pages 2, 6, 8, 22 & 23 were made by Darius Dan, Freepik, monkik and smashicons from www.flaticon.com.

Illustrations

Don Hatcher: pages 4 & 29. Simon Kneebone: pages 8 & 26. Angelo Madrid: pages 1 & 32.

Additional acknowledgements

With thanks to the Independence team: Shelley Baldry, Danielle Lobban, Jackie Staines and Jan Sunderland.

Tracy Biram

Cambridge, May 2020